Travel Guide

ISRAEL

P9-AGT-900

SUE BRYANT

NEW
HOLLAND

NEW
HOLLAND

★★★ Highly recommended
★★ Recommended
★ See if you can

Third edition published in 2006
by New Holland Publishers (UK) Ltd
London • Cape Town • Sydney • Auckland
First edition published in 1995
10 9 8 7 6 5 4 3 2

website: www.newhollandpublishers.com

Garfield House, 86 Edgware Road
London W2 2EA
United Kingdom

80 McKenzie Street
Cape Town 8001
South Africa

Unit 1, 66 Gibbes Street,
Chatswood, NSW 2067
Australia

218 Lake Road
Northcote, Auckland
New Zealand

Distributed in the USA by
The Globe Pequot Press, Connecticut

ISBN 978 1 84537 356 6

Although every effort has been made to ensure that
this guide is up to date and current at time of going
to print, the Publisher accepts no responsibility or
liability for any loss, injury or inconvenience
incurred by readers or travellers using this guide.

Keep us Current
Information in travel guides is apt to change, which
is why we regularly update our guides. We'd be
grateful to receive feedback if you've noted something we should include in our updates. If you have
new information, please share it with us by writing to
the Publishing Manager, Globetrotter, at the office
nearest to you (addresses on this page). The most
significant contribution to each new edition will
receive a free copy of the updated guide.

Publishing Manager (SA): Thea Grobbelaar
DTP Cartographic Manager: Genené Hart
Editors: Thea Grobbelaar, Tarryn Berry, Susannah
Coucher, Catherine Mallinick.
Picture Researchers: Shavonne Govender, Colleen
Abrahams, Rowena Curtis
Design and DTP: Nicole Bannister, Lellyn Creamer,
Simon Lewis, Éloise Moss.
Cartographers: Genené Hart, Nicole Bannister

Reproduction by Hirt & Carter (Pty) Ltd, Cape Town
Printed and bound by Times Offset (M) Sdn. Bhd.,
Malaysia.

Photographic Credits:
Hanan Isachar/jonarnoldimages.com, cover; **Life
File/Jane Archer**, page 88; **Life File/Mike Evans**, pages
9 (top), 11, 23 (top), 30, 35, 47, 69 (top), 71, 77, 82;
Life File/Barry Mayes, page 63; **Life File/Stuart
Norgrove**, pages 49 (top and bottom), 54; **Christine
Osborne**, pages 8, 12, 13, 19 (bottom), 20, 21 (top),
23 (bottom), 25, 27, 28 (bottom), 34, 36, 40, 41, 46,
48, 52, 56, 58 (top), 66, 75 (top and bottom), 76, 78,
79 (bottom), 85, 91, 103, 104, 107, 109; **Photobank/
Adrian Baker**, pages 36, 37, 86; **PictureBank Photo
Library**, 58 (bottom), 59, 97 (top and bottom), 117;
Mariëlle Renssen, pages 21 (bottom), 28 (top), 29, 74,
79 (top), 84, 89 (top and bottom), 90, 93, 94 (top),
118, 119 (top and bottom); **Neil Setchfield**, pages 18,
33 (bottom), 39,42, 94 (bottom), 95, 96, 112, 115,
116; **Travel Ink/Nick Battersby**, pages 24, 55; **Travel
Ink/David Forman**, pages 44, 45; **Travel Ink/Barry
Hughes**, page 9 (bottom); **Travel Ink/Julian Loader**,
page 22; **Travel Ink/Walter Wolfe**, pages 17, 64; **Peter
Wilson**, title page, pages 6, 7, 14, 15, 16, 19 (top),
26, 33 (top), 43, 69 (bottom), 70, 73, 87, 92, 100,
104, 105, 106, 108.

The author would like to thank the following for
assistance with the preparation of this book: Israel
Government Tourist Office; El Al; Dan Hotels; Vered
Hagalil; Nirvana Resort and Spa Hotel; and Ziv Cohen.

Front Cover: *Masada, one of the most spectacular
and poignant sites in Israel.*
Title Page: *The Roman settlement of Tel Beit She'an is
being painstakingly excavated.*

CONTENTS

1
Introducing
Israel

Few sights can be as stirring as **Jerusalem**'s golden Dome of the Rock glowing in the sunset, the whole of the honey-coloured city stretched out below, with wild thyme and rosemary scenting the balmy air. But Israel, a tiny strip of land clinging to the edge of the Arabian peninsula, is full of such magnificent views and unexpected contrasts.

There are the bright lights and skyscrapers of lively **Tel Aviv**; or the dazzling salt islands floating on the **Dead Sea**, shimmering in a permanent heat haze. At the northern end of the country are the lush, forested slopes of snow-capped **Mount Hermon** and the foaming rapids of the **River Jordan**, while the south promises the luxurious pleasures of **Eilat**, a thriving holiday resort on the Red Sea, on the edge of the baking **Negev Desert**.

History unravels before you in the Holy Land. Follow the pilgrims along the **Via Dolorosa** in Jerusalem's **Old City**; learn the tragic story of **Masada**, high above the **Dead Sea**; or marvel at the Dead Sea Scrolls, the oldest document known to man, in the **Israel Museum**.

Five million people from five continents have made their home here, each retaining their cultural identity, creating a colourful melting pot with a single goal, to reside and worship in the biblical land of milk and honey. Visitors flock here in their thousands, many of them on the pilgrimage of a lifetime. But even the least religiously inclined cannot fail to be moved by the magnificent landscapes, incredible history and radiant colours of this fascinating country.

TOP ATTRACTIONS

*** **Jerusalem's Old City:** thousands of years of history.
*** **Jaffa Port:** wonderful nightlife and restaurants.
*** **Masada:** 2000-year-old ruins, with a tragic story.
*** **Dead Sea:** float on the mineral-rich sea.
*** **Nazareth:** walk in the footsteps of Jesus.
*** **Sea of Galilee:** green countryside, adventure sports.
** **Akko:** explore the eerie underground Crusader city.
** **Eilat:** indulge in beach life and superb diving.

Opposite: *Traditional Bar Mitzvah celebrations at Jerusalem's Western Wall.*

GEOGRAPHY AND STATISTICS

Independence day:
14 May 1948
Members of parliament: 120
Population: Five million
Religion: 80% Jews; the
remaining 20% Muslims,
Samaritans, Christians, Druze,
Baha'i and others
Languages: Hebrew and Arabic.
English, French, German,
Yiddish, Russian, Spanish, Polish
and Hungarian also spoken
Highest point: Mount Hermon,
2224m (7296ft)
Lowest point: Dead Sea,
about –400m (–1300ft)

Right: *Turbulent on some stretches, tranquil on others, the River Jordan links the Sea of Galilee with the Dead Sea.*

ISRAEL'S H₂O

Most of Israel's water for drinking and irrigation comes from the Sea of Galilee. With two million tourists a year, salt springs, peat flows and sewage from the area to contend with, the lake's eco-system is increasingly fragile. The water is dangerously close to its 'red line', the line below which its pollutants become too concentrated for consumption. Israelis are used to conserving water and visitors should respect the notices in hotels asking them to do the same.

THE LAND

Israel is a country of incredible natural diversity. Snow-capped mountains, arid desert, green vineyards and rocky hills all fall within its compact boundaries. The country is just 418km (260 miles) from north to south and 112km (70 miles) at its widest point. Physical borders are formed by the **Mediterranean Sea** to the west, the northernmost fragments of the **Great Rift Valley** to the east, and a narrow finger of the **Red Sea** in the south. Israel shares its political borders with Lebanon, Syria, Jordan and Egypt.

Mountains and Rivers

The snow-capped **Mount Hermon** in the **Golan Heights** to the north is the country's highest point, at 2224m (7296ft). A lower, undulating range forming the Hills of Galilee, Samaria and Judea forms the spine of the north-ern end of the country. In the deep south, across the scrub-covered landscape of the **Negev Desert**, the steep hills of the Egyptian Sinai, Jordan and Saudi Arabia plunge into the Red Sea. The Negev itself, meanwhile, has an unusual geology of ancient craters, the best known of which is **Maktesh Ramon** situated in the town of Mitzpe Ramon, where interesting prehistoric remains have been found. The **Jordan River**, which links the Sea of Galilee – in reality an inland lake – with the Dead Sea, forms the lifeblood of Israel. Fed by three trib-utaries, **Nahal Hermon**, a spring at the base of Mount Hermon, **Nahal Dan** and **Nahal Senir** from the Lebanon, the river gushes into the Sea of Galilee from the north.

Seas and Shores

The **Dead Sea**, the lowest point on earth at about 400m (1300ft) below sea level, is effectively the end of the Jordan River. Intense heat at this depth causes rapid evaporation, leaving a mineral-rich soup that sustains no life. West of the central hills, the land flattens out into a fertile coastal plain, sloping gently towards the Mediterranean as well as sustaining two large cities, Tel Aviv and Haifa. The plain supports intensive agriculture. The northern end of the Mediterranean coast is a series of scenic rocky peninsulas, hidden bays and coastal mountains, purple in the heat haze. South of Caesarea, however, the shoreline flattens out into one long, straight stretch of sand that continues all the way to the Palestinian Gaza Strip in the far south.

Israel has another, tiny section of shoreline in its deep south, the highly developed resort of **Eilat**, nestling at the tip of the **Red Sea**. Eilat's beaches are carefully protected, as stunning coral reefs lie immediately offshore, just feet below the surface. This, combined with spectacular underwater life, is the reason for the Red Sea's growing popularity as a diving location.

Below: *The rocky Negev Desert covers the southern half of the country.*

Below: *A carpet of spring flowers covers the meadows around Caesarea in the north.*

Climate

Summer in Israel extends all the way from April to October, with short, mild winters from November to March. Tel Aviv and Haifa on the coast are much cooler in **summer** than inland cities, and have an average daily maximum of 30°C (86°F) in August and September, the hottest months, whilst Eilat swelters in 40°C (104°F). The coast and the Jordan River Valley are very humid.

In the north, **winters** are cool with January temperatures dropping to around 6°C (42°F) in Jerusalem and sometimes lower, causing ground frost. Mount Hermon in the Golan Heights is actually a ski resort, while at the same time visitors to the Dead Sea can enjoy daytime highs of 22°C (72°F) in February. Rainfall is low here, even in winter, and the spring showers that feed the Jordan River are vital to the country's water supply.

Plant Life

Thanks to its incredibly diverse landscape, Israel supports an astonishing variety of animals and plants. This

was not always the case; under the rule of the Ottoman Turks, mass deforestation meant the land became a dust bowl and many birds and mammals became extinct. The Jewish National Fund has set up a huge reforestation programme (this was started in the 1950s) which has resulted in 10% of the country's land area being covered with trees. In addition, the **Hai-Bar programme** aims to bring back biblical creatures such as the **Addax antelope**, the wild **Asiatic ass** (once ridden by Jesus), the **Mesopotamian fallow deer**, the exquisite **white oryx** (the creature which spawned the myth of the unicorn) and even **ostrich** to the land of the Bible. This means that more and more rare wild animals are being released in Israel's 280 nature reserves. Elsewhere, mainly deep in the desert or mountains, **gazelle** and **ibex** thrive, as do foxes, wolves and, around Mount Hermon, otters.

Beautiful forests of **Eurasian oak**, **African acacia** and the native **Jerusalem pine** now cover Israel's soil with oleander, myrtle and fragrant wild herbs flourishing in the drier areas. Cultivated trees include apricot, almond, citrus and walnut, while more unexpected country scenes include alpine meadows on the slopes of Mount Hermon and the world's northernmost papyrus swamp at nearby Hula. As far back as the 11th century, 'biblical' flowers were prized as souvenirs and many have become extinct, but the beautiful **Madonna lily** (an alpine meadow species) can still be found.

Wildlife

Hundreds of species of migratory birds pass Israel en route from Europe to Africa, among them storks, herons, ducks, pelicans, hawks, gulls, waders, plovers, sandpipers, flamingos and song birds. Once every seven years, when the vineyards outside Tel Aviv are left fallow according to kosher law, the birds enjoy a free bonanza of ripe grapes. The best place to view these migrants is at **Eilat** in the far south, considered by ornithologists to be among the Mediterranean region's finest spots for bird-watching.

Above: *Camels are a regular means of transport for Bedouin people.*

BIRD-WATCHING CALENDAR

Sep–Oct is the best time for observing the **migration** of predatory birds, storks and pelicans in the Hula Valley. Waterfowl are abundant from Nov–Feb, while the migratory birds return to the north in Mar–Apr. Malagan Michael Nature Reserve is open from Nov–Mar for observation of waterfowl, while Feb–May and Aug–Oct are the best times to enjoy the spectacular migration over Eilat. The North Beach and the salt ponds are a bird-watcher's dream, and viewing times are best in the early morning or late afternoon.

Below: *Bee-eaters are among the bird species to be seen.*

HISTORICAL CALENDAR

12,000BC Cave-dwellers in Carmel.

7500BC First settlement, Jericho.

3200BC Canaanite tribes establish fortified cities.

2200–1500BC Abraham arrives in Canaan and founds Hebrew race.

1550–1200BC Exodus from Egypt. Delivery of Ten Commandments (Mount Sinai).

1000BC Jerusalem becomes capital of 12 tribes of Israel.

722BC Northern Kingdom falls to Assyrians; Israelis exiled.

332–37BC Hellenistic period.

37BC–AD324 Birth and crucifixion of Jesus. Jewish uprisings against Rome. Fall of Masada (AD73).

4th Century Christianity becomes official religion of Roman Empire.

AD622 Birth of Islam; Muslim Arabs conquer Middle East.

AD637 Jerusalem surrenders to Arabs.

1096–1204 Christian Crusaders; Jews massacred.

1291–1917 Ottoman Turkish rule.

1889 Opening of Suez Canal revives trade routes.

1897 First Zionist World Congress.

1914–18 World War I. Britain promises Palestinian Jews and Arabs liberation from Ottoman Empire.

1917–48 British Mandate. Jewish immigration to Palestine restricted. Six million Jews murdered by the Nazis in World War II.

1948 State of Israel proclaimed. Immediate invasion by Arab armies.

1967 The Six-Day War.

1973 Yom Kippur War.

1977 Egypt and Israel sign Camp David Accord.

1985 Israeli Defence Forces withdraw from Lebanon.

1987 Intifada, the Palestinian uprising. Terrorist attacks.

1990–91 Gulf War; PLO backs Iraq. Tel Aviv bombed.

1993 Peace agreement signed between Yitzhak Rabin and Yasser Arafat of the PLO. Jericho and Gaza Strip returned to Palestinians.

1994 Land border with Jordan opens at Eilat.

1995 Rabin assassinated.

1999 Likud Party elected.

2000 Second Intifada.

2001 Ariel Sharon elected prime minister.

2005 Israeli settlers withdraw from Gaza.

Opposite: *Stunning frescoes can be seen inside Jerusalem's Tower of David. The tower contains the Museum of the History of Jerusalem, detailing aspects of the story of one of the world's most contested cities.*

HISTORY IN BRIEF

Situated at the crossroad of two continents, Africa and Asia, and passed by all the great trade routes of the ancient world, it was inevitable that the tiny sliver of land now called Israel should play a dramatic role in world history. Its physical location, combined with the belief of three great religions – Christianity, Judaism and Islam – that Israel was their spiritual home, has inspired 4000 years of struggle over the land of milk and honey.

In the Beginning

Evidence of cave dwellers around **Carmel** has been dated back to 600,000 years before Christ. **Jericho**, one of the oldest cities in the world, was settled about 7000BC, while archaeologists have discovered that **Be'er Sheva** was inhabited in 3200BC. People lived in small villages where they grew crops, farmed animals, made simple tools from copper and bronze and followed pagan religious beliefs.

The Land of Canaan

By 3000BC, Canaanite tribes had established fortified cities in this land which bordered the two great powers of the time, **Egypt** and **Assyria**, both of whom indulged in frequent, vicious battles along the Mediterranean trade route. New tribes began to arrive; belonging to one of them was the patriarch **Abraham**, believed to have come from Ur in what is now Iraq and to have fathered the Israeli people.

Although the only record of Abraham and his sons **Isaac** and **Jacob** is in the Bible (there is a possibility that Abraham himself was a mythical figure), there was certainly a leader of the Israelite tribe who, unlike the other tribes of the time, worshipped a single deity.

By the 13th century BC, Egypt had been weakened in the north by its war with the **Hittite Empire**, a feature of North Syria and Asia Minor during the second millennium BC, and gradually new, smaller powers including Abraham's descendants, the **Israelites**, began to emerge.

The Israelites and the Promised Land

According to the Bible, Abraham's descendants were taken into slavery in Egypt around 1550BC. The **Book of Exodus** tells how they escaped under the leadership of **Moses**, made a miraculous 40-year journey across the wilderness and the Red Sea, and received the **Ten Commandments** on **Mount Sinai** before conquering their Promised Land.

The **Israelites** settled in what is now Israel during the early Iron Age (1200BC) and formed a monarchy, headed by **King Saul** whose adopted son and successor, David, led them to final victory over the Philistines, an aggressive

THE BOOK OF EXODUS

The *Book of Exodus* is one of history's great adventure stories. It tells the story of God choosing Moses to lead the 'Children of Israel' out of slavery in Egypt. Ten plagues are inflicted on the Egyptians and the waters of the Red Sea part to allow the fleeing Israelites to cross. Subsequently, in Sinai, while the Israelites are wandering in the wilderness, Moses encounters the burning bush. God then gives Moses the Ten Commandments and the Israelites build the Tabernacle on Mount Sinai into which are placed various sacred furnishings, among them the **Ark of the Covenant**. The Jewish feast of **Sukkot** today recreates the conditions of the wilderness as families eat under temporary shelters outside their homes.

ELIJAH'S CHALLENGE

Elijah was a popular Hebrew prophet, famous for his struggle against Ahab, the king who worshipped Baal, the Phoenician god. According to the Bible, Elijah challenged the pagans to a contest of 'miracles' and stated that only he could command the rain. After three years of drought, Elijah assembled the people of Israel on Mount Carmel and said that he had proved his point. The Baal-worshippers were killed and sure enough, the rains came.

race still controlling the coast. Saul himself secured many military victories but it was David who conquered **Jerusalem**, proclaiming it the capital of the 12 tribes of Israel. He installed the **Ark of the Covenant** (which contains the scrolls of the Torah) in the Temple of Jerusalem where the Ten Commandments are also found.

By the time of **King Solomon** (950BC), Israel was a powerful land, stretching from the **Red Sea** to the **Euphrates River** in the north. But jealousies between tribes led to 10 in the north forming the **Kingdom of Israel**, while the tribes of Judah and Benjamin formed the southern Kingdom of Judea. Alliances with neighbours continued to be formed and broken until the northern kingdom fell in 722BC to invading Assyria.

Babylonian and Persian Rule

The Israelites from the north were exiled overseas and gradually became absorbed into other societies. The south held out for a further 150 years until the **Babylonians**, who had replaced the Assyrians in power, invaded in 586BC. The Babylonian army crushed Judah, and destroyed the Temple of Jerusalem. The surviving population was exiled to Babylonia, where they mourned for their lost land.

As foretold by the prophets of the time, the Babylonian Empire fell to **Persians** 40 years later and the exiles were allowed to return. The Temple of Jerusalem was rebuilt but tension ran high between the **Jews** (from Judah) and the **Samaritans,** those northerners who had stayed in Israel and married foreign immigrants brought in by the Assyrians.

Below: *Israel's countryside is dotted with ancient tools like this wheat grinding stone.*

Roman Times

Alexander the Great defeated the **Persians** in 333BC and for 900 years, Israel was part of the **Greco-Roman Empire**. Hellenic rulers attempted to outlaw Judaism in the 2nd century BC, defiling the Temple in the process. Jewish sovereignty was then re-established, but lasted only until 63BC, when the country was annexed by the **Romans**

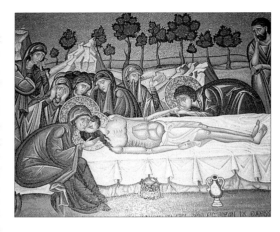

Above: *The life and crucifixion of Christ is told in frescoes inside the Church of the Holy Sepulchre.*

and renamed Judea. **Jesus** was born – and died – at a time when Jews were split into different factions: the wealthy **Sadducees**; the **Pharisees**; the **Essenes**; and fanatical **Zealots**.

United by a hatred for the Romans, the Jews revolted in AD66, only to be crushed three years later. The Temple was destroyed and the final Jewish Zealot stronghold, **Masada**, fell in AD73 with the mass suicide of its inhabitants. The Jewish population that remained around Galilee in the north rebelled again in AD132 but was broken once and for all by the Romans' sheer numbers. Villages were destroyed and many Jews were sold into slavery.

Diaspora

The Jews scattered far and wide, from Egypt to Eastern Europe, where they worked as traders. This became known as the **Diaspora**, the Greek word for 'dispersion'. As **Christianity** became the official religion of the Roman Empire in AD4, widespread hostilities against Jews began again, although a community in Babylon, away from the Christian areas, continued to thrive.

In the 7th century the Muslim religion, **Islam**, was founded by the prophet Mohammed. After receiving his first revelation in AD616, Mohammed taught in Mecca,

CRUSADER CASTLE

One of the most picturesque of the Crusader castles, Nimrod's Fortress stands like a fairy-tale vision on the slopes of Mount Hermon near the Golan Heights, in the north of Israel, and is surrounded by thick forest. From the crumbling towers and walls, there are impressive views of the flat Hula Valley to the south and the mountain pass between Hermon and Syria. Not surprisingly, the fortress once served as a highway stronghold along the road to Damascus but was abandoned after the fall of the Second Crusader Kingdom in 1291.

Above: *Early mosaic map representing part of Palestine.*

his teachings forming the basis of the Koran, Islam's sacred scripture. He was forced to flee to Medina in 622, but returned with his followers to conquer Mecca in 630, becoming the recognized prophet of Arabia.

Fuelled by this new religion, an Arab invasion took place in AD640, their army storming across what was then Palestine and conquering it. Palestine became part of Syria and Jerusalem was declared a Holy City by the Muslims. The great mosque, the **Dome of the Rock**, was built in 691.

Crusades

Christians in Europe viewed the Arab rule of the Holy Land as an insult, and in the 11th century the Pope ordered a series of Crusades, which by 1099 had effectively reconquered Jerusalem, though thousands of Muslims and Jews were slaughtered in the process. After the **Second Crusade** (1147–49) Jews were allowed back into Jerusalem, but the **Third** and **Fourth Crusades**, ending in 1204, were particularly vicious and anti-Semitic, branding Jews as 'God-killers'.

In 1187 Saladin, the ruler of Egypt, managed to rout the Crusaders at the Horns of Hittim. A series of disastrous campaigns was carried out by the Crusaders in an attempt to recoup their losses but in 1291 the Crusader kingdom finally came to an end with the fall of Akko, when the Crusaders were defeated by the Mamelukes who had succeeded Saladin as rulers of Egypt.

Ottoman Turkish Rule

Over the next 300 years, Palestine was ruled by the military **Mameluke regime**. Trade routes and pilgrimages dried up as the world's attention focused on the

---

THE FATHER OF ZIONISM

Born in May 1860 in Budapest, Theodor Herzl is regarded as the father of Zionism. He studied law in Vienna but ended up following a career as a journalist and playwright. Herzl grew increasingly concerned about the rise of anti-Semitism in Vienna in the 1880s – the initial motivation in Zionism was not to preserve a religion, but simply to protect Jewish people. In 1896 he published *The Jewish State*, a guide to creating a refuge for Jews. In 1897, he organized the first World Zionist Congress in Basel, Switzerland, and set up a Jewish Colonial Trust. He continued to lobby internationally for a home for the world's Jews until his death in 1904.

newly discovered Americas, and the land of milk and honey became a barren backwater. In 1517, the Mamelukes were defeated by the **Ottoman Turks**. Under their **Suleiman the Magnificent** (1520–66), prosperity returned to the Holy Land, lasting until the decline of the Ottoman Empire in the 18th century.

A foray by **Napoleon** in 1799 into Akko (now Acre) sparked European interest in Palestine. The Russians built a complex west of Jerusalem to house Russian Orthodox pilgrims, while Europeans set up small colonies to protect the city's Latin Christians (Roman Catholics). In 1889 the opening of the **Suez Canal** re-established trade routes in the Middle East.

Birth of Zionism

Meanwhile, life continued to be tough for the Jewish exiles. The pogroms, or mass persecution, of the Jews in Russia, which caused tens of thousands of Jews to flee yet again – some of them to Palestine – gave rise to a new feeling: **Zionism**. This was the call for the establishment of a Jewish state in Palestine, first dreamed of by the Russian-born journalist Peretz Smolenskin. The idea was brought together by a Viennese journalist and playwright **Theodor Herzl** (1860–1904), who lobbied the influential to find a home for the scattered Jewish people. He published a document, *The Jewish State*, in 1896 and established the World Zionist Congress in 1897.

British Mandate

The Ottoman Empire had been crumbling and by the end of World War I (1914–18) Palestine was no longer controlled by the Turks. In 1920 the League of Nations granted Britain a mandate to govern Palestine and another wave of Jews quickly returned to the Holy Land

> **THE SCROLLS OF HISTORY**
>
> The Scrolls were discovered in 1947 by a Bedouin shepherd, who was looking for a lost goat around the shores of the Dead Sea. In the ruined, mountainous settlement of Qumran, once inhabited by the devout Essene people, the Bedouin threw a stone into a cave and heard the sound of pottery being smashed. Further investigation revealed earthenware jars filled with flaking parchment, dating between 100BC and AD100. Subsequent explorations revealed more scrolls and many fragments of pottery, most of which are now housed in the **Israel Museum**.

Below: *For centuries, many Jews lived in crowded ghetto conditions in eastern Europe.*

Above: *The Yad Vashem Memorial in Jerusalem serves as a stark reminder of the Holocaust.*

IMMIGRANT WITH A VISION

Eliezer Ben-Yehuda was one of the original immigrants to Israel at the turn of the century and the pioneer of the modern Hebrew language. Not content with reviving his homeland, Ben-Yehuda was determined to rejuvenate the ancient language of the Bible and in the early days was a peculiar sight, conducting his daily business in the ancient biblical tongue. He went to tremendous effort to bring up his children with Hebrew as their mother tongue, a fact which psychologists continue to marvel at. Ben-Yehuda devoted his life to modernizing the language and the result was a fairly uncomplicated version, which was easy for the thousands of immigrants flooding into the country to learn.

---

with new hope in their hearts. For those who had been part of the first wave of immigrants in the 1880s, times had been very hard, though a coordinated effort by German lawyer, **Arthur Ruppin**, to manage the funds collected for resettlement had established new towns, among them Tel Aviv. Much-neglected land, owned by absentee Arabs, was sold to the Jews, who formed workers' collectives known as **kibbutzim** to drain the malarial swamps, work the coastal plains and make Palestine a prosperous region again.

The State of Israel

Waves of refugees continued to descend on Palestine, threatened by the appointment of **Adolf Hitler** as chancellor of Germany in 1933. There was increasing unrest and uprising by Palestinian Arabs, themselves nervous of the growing Jewish power in Palestine.

The British clamped down on immigration, divided between support of the Jews and their need to maintain economic relations with the Arabs. During World War II (1939–45), six million Jews were exterminated by the Nazis, yet the terrified refugees who tried to immigrate after the **Holocaust** continued to be turned away.

Under Prime Minister Menachem Begin, Palestinian Jews rose up to form a provisional government, desperate to grant the refugees sanctuary. But refugee boats were still turned away. In disgust, the **Haganah**, an underground Jewish army, resorted to blowing up nine bridges in Palestine. The British arrested 3000 Jews and in retaliation, Begin's **Irgun** movement planted bombs in the British headquarters, the **King David Hotel** in Jerusalem, killing 91 people. In 1947 the **United Nations** were called in to resolve the problem and a plan was drawn up to partition Palestine into a Jewish and an Arab state. The Arabs were outraged.

The independent **State of Israel** was proclaimed on 14 May 1948 by Prime Minister **David Ben-Gurion**.

Almost immediately, though, the celebrations ended as six Arab states invaded the new country. In the ensuing seven-month **War of Independence**, Israel came out victorious but at the cost of 6000 lives. In 1949, Israel was admitted to the United Nations.

In July 1950, the **Law of Return** was passed by the first **Knesset** (parliament), granting all Jews the right to Israel citizenship. More waves of immigration followed and more kibbutzim were established. The new State of Israel remained a cause of concern to the Arab world, so much so, that Nasser (Egypt's new president) nationalized and assumed control of the Suez Canal which had been developed as a private company in which Britain and France were the majority shareholders. France and Britain took military action in 1956 and in the course of events Israel extended her borders, claiming the Gaza Strip and the Sinai as hers. These territories, however, were relinquished to Egypt in the ceasefire agreement between the European powers.

The Six-Day War

Israel continued to be harassed by the Arabs in the 1960s, as the USSR chose to supply arms to Egypt and Jordan, whilst Britain, France and the USA allied themselves with Israel. In a sudden move, Egypt blocked the Tiran Straits in 1967 and moved units into the Sinai. As it was clear that the Arab armies had amassed on all of Israel's borders, Israel braced itself for attack. Under the leadership of General Moshe Dayan, an Israeli pre-emptive strike annihilated the Arab armies in six days flat, establishing Israel's military supremacy in the Middle East. The Six-Day War resulted in the exodus of large numbers of Palestinians from Israel.

> ### DESERT TOMBS
>
> Israel's first prime minister, David Ben-Gurion, is buried in modest surroundings, deep in the Negev Desert, alongside his wife, Paula, close to the kibbutz where they spent their later years. Their tomb is in a national park (situated on the edge of an escarpment) where local stone and flora blend harmoniously into the barren wastes of the surrounding desert. The tomb is worth a visit for its superb views alone.

Below: *An eternal flame burns at Yad Vashem; an estimated six million Jews died in the Holocaust.*

Above: *The imposing Knesset in Jerusalem is Israel's parliament.*

The Yom Kippur War

Israel now controlled the **West Bank**, the **Gaza Strip**, the **Golan Heights**, **East Jerusalem** and the **Sinai** peninsula, all inhabited by Palestinian Arabs. Egypt, for one, refused to accept defeat and in 1973 on **Yom Kippur** they stormed the Suez Canal border, taking Israel by surprise. Israel pushed the Egyptians back, though **Golda Meir's** Labour Party never recovered financially and in 1977 Israel voted in Menachem Begin's Likuel Party.

A Kind of Peace

In 1977, Egypt's President Anwar Sadat announced a desire for peace, and soon Begin extended the first olive branch to Sadat. In 1979 the **Camp David Accords** were signed and Israel traded the Sinai for peace.

However, war with **Lebanon** and terrorist attacks by the **Palestine Liberation Organization** (PLO) continued until 1985, when the last Israeli Defence Forces withdrew from Lebanon. A tentative peace settled for two years until **Intifada**, a Palestinian uprising in Gaza and the West Bank, occurred. During the **Gulf War** (1990–91), the PLO sided with Iraq, and Israel feared attack by chemical weapons. Conventional missiles did hit Tel Aviv but Israel's lack of retaliation led to the establishment of diplomatic relations with a number of countries. In September 1993 a new peace agreement was signed between **Yitzhak Rabin** and **Yasser Arafat** of the PLO. Under these **Oslo Accords**, Jericho and the Gaza Strip were granted Palestinian autonomy. Further cities were handed back to the Palestinians in 1994. In the same year, land borders opened between Jordan and Eilat in the south. However, Yitzhak Rabin was assassinated in November 1995 and September 1996 saw further uprisings in Hebron and the Gaza Strip. The right wing Likuel Party, led by Binyamin Netanyahu, was elected in 1998 but ousted in 1999 by Ehudbarak's Likud Party after failing to show commitment to the Peace Process. Ariel

TERRORISM IN ISRAEL

There are no guarantees behind Israel's green lines (otherwise known as the Occupied Territories). These include the West Bank, the Golan Heights, East Jerusalem and the Gaza Strip, where withdrawal of Israeli settlers took place in 2005. There is a high threat of terrorism including suicide bombers in the country and Occupied Territories. Israeli cars have yellow plates, while those in the Occupied Territories have blue plates, so a car is an obvious target. Tourist buses, however, tend to be ignored and are the safest way to see the sights. For the adventurous, the United Nations in Jerusalem will arrange tours of the Palestinian refugee camps.

Sharon, elected prime minister in 2001, has had a rocky journey on the so-called 'Road Map' to peace. A second Intifada took place in 2000, since when there has been continuing violence in the Occupied Territories. A major step towards peace was taken in 2005, with the withdrawal of Israeli settlers from Gaza.

GOVERNMENT AND ECONOMY

Israel is a multiparty parliamentary democracy. The **Knesset** (parliament) of 120 members is elected by proportional representation from party lists, rather than individual candidates.

The new leader of the party or coalition that has the greatest chance of forming a government, usually with an absolute majority, is invited by the existing president to do so. The prime minister's election is slightly different, decided by separate universal vote. The president of state, meanwhile, is elected by the Knesset every five years by secret ballot. The presidency is the highest office in Israel and the president is considered to be above day-to-day politics but he does appoint judges to the Supreme Court, which is the safeguard of the country's democracy. The Supreme Court has the authority to intervene at all levels of life in Israel, from politics to economic matters, and is held in enormous respect by the people. Israelis are obsessed with politics and lively political debate is part of everyday life, so be prepared to join in.

Israel has suffered from high inflation in the past, some due to the cost of maintaining its defence force; the country has one of the proportionally highest defence budgets in the world. The economy, which switched from agricultural to post-industrial owing to its lack of natural resources, is relatively stable now but life for the visitor is not cheap. Metals and machinery make up some 39% of exports, followed by polished diamonds (24%), chemicals, rubber and plastics (19%) and to a lesser extent, food, textiles and minerals. The country's income includes US$2 billion from tourism (over 2 million tourists were expected to visit Israel in 2005), US$2 billion from the World Jewry and US$3 billion from US aid. Germany

ECONOMY: FACTS AND FIGURES

Gross Domestic Product: US$129 billion
GDP growth rate: 3.9%
Inflation: 0%
Foreign trade: US$34.41 billion visible exports; US$36.84 billion imports.
Main trading partners: European Community, USA, Hong Kong.

Above: *Unexploded mines still lie in the Golan Heights.*
Below: *Israel's flag bears the Star of David.*

SERVING THEIR COUNTRY

The Israeli Defence Force (IDF) is a source of national pride. All men and women are required at the age of 18 to do National Service. For men, this service lasts for three years but women are only required to do two years. From an even earlier age young people are assessed according to their suitability for divisions such as the para-troops, the Air Force or the infantry and tank corps. A career in the army is con-sidered highly prestigious and it's a matter of considerable pride among many senior civilians that they once held posts as officers.

Opposite bottom: *Jewish people pray at the West-ern Wall of Jerusalem.*
Below: *Orthodox Jewish boys outside their synagogue school.*

pays US$500 million a year to Israel in compensation for Nazi atrocities. Unemployment is around 10%, not helped by the continuing influx of skilled Russian Jews.

THE PEOPLE

If there was ever a cultural melting pot, Israel is it. Under the **Law of Return**, any Jew, anywhere in the world, has the right to live in Israel and take Israeli citizenship. This is what has brought wave after wave of immigrants, from the first Russians who arrived in 1882 to Germans, North Africans and now, an estimated one million Soviet Jews, looking for a new life in the sun after years of poverty under Communism.

Israel's population, including the Occupied Territories of Judea and Samaria, is around 6.3 million. More than four-fifths are Jews, with 750,000 Muslims and the rest Christians, Druze and others. While all these immigrants live and worship alongside one another, cultural boundaries remain clear and visitors will encounter second-generation Armenians and Ethiopians who still speak as though they've just arrived in the country.

Native-born Israelis are nicknamed **sabras** – a cactus fruit which is tough and thorny on the outside and sweet on the inside – but in reality, Israelis are incredibly hospitable and naturally curious about visitors. Family ties are strong in Israel, and in Jewish families Friday nights are spent at home. Children are welcomed everywhere and usually stay up quite late.

Israelis are not big drinkers. A more typical night out consists of drinking coffee and talking. Young people are surprisingly mature, thanks to their three years' compulsory national service (two for girls), and tend to be great travellers and lovers of the outdoors.

Israeli people in general are hard-working, aggressive in business and highly demonstrative: shouting and gesticulating doesn't necessarily mean anger but discussion. Israelis are also immersed in politics, which is discussed endlessly on the radio and TV and in the many daily newspapers. By all means enter into a political discussion, but remember to have your argument well prepared.

Language

The diversity of the population is reflected in the number of languages you'll hear on the streets: **Hebrew**, **Yiddish**, **English**, **German**, **Arabic**, **French**, **Spanish**, **Amharic** (spoken by Ethiopian Jews) and a lot of **Russian**, spoken by recently arrived immigrants who now account for one-fifth of the population. Israel Radio broadcasts in 12 different languages. Hebrew and Arabic, however, are the official languages, with English widely understood. Hebrew today is actually similar to biblical Hebrew, with an expanded vocabulary and a few English words thrown in. While the visitor can get by in virtually any language, it is only polite – and much appreciated by the locals – to learn a few words of Hebrew.

Few foreign language television programmes are dubbed, so if you're learning Hebrew, watching TV is a perfect way to practise reading. Alternatively, there is plenty of choice in reading matter. Israel has 26 daily newspapers, more than any other country in the world, published in Hebrew, Arabic, Russian and English. For English-speaking visitors, *The Jerusalem Post* is a good, if rather right-wing read.

Above: *Muslim traders sell grapes outside Jerusalem's Old City.*

LANGUAGE OF THE EUROPEANS

Yiddish is a Germanic language written in Hebrew characters and spoken in Israel by the older generation, particularly those with European roots. The language developed in southwestern Germany between the 9th and 12th centuries, as Hebrew words that pertained to Jewish religious life were added to German. Later, as Jews moved eastward into Slavic-speaking areas, some Slavic influences were added, in addition to Romanian, French and several English words. In the early years of the 20th century Yiddish was spoken by an estimated 11 million people in Eastern Europe and the USA, although the extermination of so many Jews in the Holocaust led to its decline.

SAMARITANS

The handful of Samaritans left in Israel today are descended from those mentioned in the Bible. By the time the Jews returned from Babylon, the Samaritans, who had stayed, had intermarried with the invaders and, while they adhered to the Jewish faith, were looked down on for not being pure. Strong antipathy arose between the two groups. The holiest site for Samaritans today is Mount Gerizim, where they once had a temple, later destroyed by the Hasmoneans. During Samaritan Passover, lambs are sacrificed here, although non-Samaritan spectators are asked to leave for the ritual.

Below: *Israel is the spiritual home to many religions, including Greek Orthodox.*

Religion

As well as forming the spiritual home of Judaism, Israel is the world's most important Christian site and is of great significance to Muslims. Israel is also home to Samaritans, Armenians, Eastern Orthodox, Druze and forms the world headquarters of the Baha'i. Freedom of worship is guaranteed and, whatever your faith, you will be welcome. Of Israel's five million inhabitants, some four million are Jewish and only 20% of these claim to be 'practising' Jews, which means: daily prayer, religious observance of the Sabbath and keeping a kosher household.

Shabbat (the Sabbath) – sundown on Friday to sundown on Saturday – is a time of rest, contemplation and prayer and is strictly observed: exact times of sunset are published in the newspapers. Shops and restaurants close, offices are deserted, and public transport stops except in Tel Aviv and, to an extent, Haifa. In religious households, people don't cook or switch on any appliance, although nowadays electric timers are used to operate lights and food is prepared the day before and kept warm.

On Friday nights, traditional Shabbat supper is served. At sunset on Saturday, a *Havdalah* candle is lit to mark the passing of the holy day and a blessing is read. The family drinks a glass of kosher wine and passes round a pot of sweet-smelling spices for everybody to inhale.

Shabbat need not affect the visitor. Chinese and Arab restaurants stay open and there is plenty of activity in the big hotels. In Tel Aviv, after supper, huge crowds turn out to stroll along the promenade in the warm night air.

Men in long black coats and black hats, with peculiar locks of hair around their faces, belong to the ultra-orthodox sect, the devout **Hassidic Jews** who still dress as their original Eastern European predecessors did 200 years ago. They live in ghettos, the largest of which is Me'a She'arim in Jerusalem, almost re-

THE SECT OF MYSTERY

The Druze are a mysterious sect of around 60,000 people, living in the mountains around Carmel, and are descended from an Egyptian religious movement of some 900 years ago. The men dress distinctively in a white headdress, black bloomers and cummerbund and they sport bushy moustaches. No-one knows exactly what Druze beliefs entail as they have been kept a secret through the generations, although reincarnation does play a part. Despite their enigmatic air, Druze are successfully integrated into Israeli society and unlike some sects – the Hassidim, for example – serve their time in the Israeli Defence Force.

creating the conditions of the Eastern Europe they left behind, with narrow alleys and high, forbidding walls. Many of them do not serve in the army – a source of great irritation to Israelis – and furthermore, do not work, preferring to study the Old Testament instead.

Strangely, a number of Hassidic Jews do not even believe in the State of Israel. Their doctrine insists that the State of Israel will only exist after the coming of the Messiah, which they believe has not yet happened. Visitors to Me'a She'arim are politely warned at the entrance to dress with extreme modesty.

Above left: *Muslims turn towards Mecca for the call to prayer.*
Below: *Study of the Torah, the holy book, is part of every practising Jew's upbringing.*

Festivals and Holidays

With so many different religions practised, life in Israel seems like one long holiday. Christians observe Christmas and Easter, Muslims Ramadan and Jews the 13 holidays on the Jewish Calendar, which are 'official' as far as shops and businesses are concerned. But Israelis will also celebrate New Year's Eve. The **Hebrew calendar** is based on the lunar year, so holiday dates do not follow the Gregorian calendar. God is said to have created the Earth in 3760BC, which corresponds to the Gregorian year 0. Thus 1998 is the year 5758, and so on.

Above: *Worshippers observe the religious holiday of Yom Kippur.*

Rosh Hashanah and Yom Kippur

Jewish New Year – Rosh Hashanah, or **Days of Judgement** – falls in September or October. As the only two-day public holiday, this is the time when Israelis head for the beach, the Sea of Galilee or the mountains. For the religious, this is a time of self-examination. Ten days later is the **Day of Atonement**, or Yom Kippur, which is the holiest day of the year. Everything stops while the religious fast from sunset to sunset, and spend the day in the synagogue.

Sukkot and Simchat Torah

Sukkot, the **Harvest Festival**, is only a week or so after Yom Kippur. Every family builds a *succah*, a temporary shelter made of palm branches and leaves. Under its roof the family eats for seven days, commemorating the structures under which the Israelites lived during the exodus from Egypt. On the fifth day, there are parades and walks around Jerusalem. The last of the autumn vacations, the **Rejoicing of the Torah** (the first five books of the Bible), means singing and dancing in the streets with the **Torah Scroll**.

Hanukkah

The Feast of Lights in December celebrates the ancient Israelites' revolt against the Greeks, who tried to suppress the Jewish faith. Hanukkah candles are lit on a *menorah*, the seven – or eight – branched candelabra owned by every household. Small jelly-filled doughnuts are eaten everywhere, and children enjoy parties and games.

Passover

Passover, or Pesach, in March or April, celebrates the liberation of the ancient Israelites from Egypt. No bread or yeast is eaten for a week – just unleavened *matzot* – and people rid their houses of anything containing yeast, an excuse for a good spring clean. The Passover dinner, or *seder*, is a feast symbolizing the experiences of the Israelites as they fled from Egypt, including bitter herbs representing the bitterness of slavery.

Traditional Cultures

Dance, art and theatre are prolific in Israel and there are cultural performances everywhere, from the smallest kibbutz to the theatre stages of Jerusalem and Tel Aviv. As well as classical ballet, dance incorporates several ethnic styles, such as Hassidic, Arabic and Yemenite folk dancing. **Bat-Sheva** and **Bat-Dor** are both modern dance companies that perform regularly in the cities of Jerusalem and Tel Aviv.

The Arts

Israel's magnificent landscapes have inspired countless painters and there are large artistic communities in **Jaffa**, the village of **Ein Hod** near Haifa and **Safed** in the Galilee region. Important galleries include the **Israel Museum** in Jerusalem, which houses works of contemporary Israeli art, Jewish European art and sculpture, a vast number of European works and a modern section. In Tel Aviv, don't miss the **Helena Rubenstein Pavilion**, the collections of which include European and American art from the 17th to the 20th centuries.

The Israel Philharmonic Orchestra is world famous and often features well-known guest performers. The orchestra's home is the **Mann Auditorium** in Tel Aviv and tickets are usually hard to come by. Instead, try to see the **Jerusalem Symphony Orchestra**, which performs weekly throughout the winter. Haifa and Rishon le-Zion both have good symphony orchestras, too.

Rock Around Israel

Almost all Israeli music, from folk to rock to classical, has political overtones, with war and a longing for peace as common themes for songs. But much of the music, with its sombre lyrics, is pleasant enough and visitors will encounter home-grown punk, rock and rap as well as imports. Popular Israeli singers include Shlomo Artsi, famous for his ballads; rock group Tipex; musician Yehuda Poliker; ballad singer Hava Alberstein; and Rivka Zohar. Free concerts often take place in Jerusalem, Tel Aviv and the coastal resorts and in any case, the visitor should try to experience some folk dancing and singing.

Below: *An Armenian woman in Jerusalem crafts intricate examples of ceramicware.*

Above: *Relaxing at the sunny resort of Eilat by the Red Sea.*

Nothing quite beats the romance of theatre at dusk in the beautiful Roman amphitheatre at **Caesarea** as the sun sets across the waves. Try to see something of the Festival of Music and Drama which takes place here and in **Beit She'an** in the Galilee area each May. Otherwise, there are regular theatre productions in the **Habima Theatre** in Tel Aviv and **Haifa Municipal Theatre**, mainly in Hebrew though occasionally plays are produced in English or Yiddish.

Also worth a visit is the **Red Sea Jazz Festival** in August and the **Akko Fringe Theatre Festival** in September. Spring brings the Rubenstein Piano Competition, attracting talent from all over the world, and in Haifa, there is the colourful **International Folk Festival**.

Nightlife

Tel Aviv has the liveliest nightlife, with plenty of bars, nightclubs and jazz cafés. The ancient fishing port of **Jaffa** is the best place for bar-crawling and simply wandering around. Pop concerts are held in Tel Aviv's **HaYarkon Park**, under the stars. **Jerusalem** is less exciting for clubbing but has a lively café society, while **Haifa** has some great areas for people-watching. **Eilat**, meanwhile, is a more typical holiday resort with a mixture of clubs and pubs focusing on the big hotels on North Beach.

Sport in Israel

Israelis are generally active, outdoor types and there are countless opportunities to indulge in sports from the everyday to the extreme.

Hiking is very popular, some of the best areas being the Negev Desert and the Galilee region. In the Negev, there are marked trails in the national parks like Ein Gedi, overlooking the Dead Sea, although many locals prefer to hike away from the tourist areas, camping out overnight. **Mountain biking**, rappelling and off-road driving are all popular in this area, too.

Around the Sea of Galilee, there are gentle walking trails taking in the religious sites and others covering more remote areas, including the spectacular Golan Heights. A guide is essential outside the designated park areas on the Golan Heights as danger still exists from unexploded landmines.

Watersports abound around the lake, from water ski-ing to canoeing. **White-water rafting** is popular on the River Jordan, which is rated as one of the most exciting in the world. For a gentler experience, try **inner tubing**; in other words, drifting down a quiet stretch of the river sitting in a rubber tube, soaking up the peace and quiet.

Horse riding is also very popular and some of the best rides are from ranches located around the lake. Horses tend to be trained Western-style and many have thoroughbred blood.

A visit to Eilat is an ideal opportunity to try **scuba diving** in the Red Sea's warm, clear waters with their spectacular coral reefs. A starter course takes just one day. For those who prefer not to dive, the snorkelling is almost as good. On the Mediter-ranean coast, meanwhile, sea kayaking and sailing are popular sports.

Below: *Israel is full of sporting opportunities; in Tel Aviv you can windsurf off the white-sand beach.*

Above: *One of Jerusalem's many popular bakeries.*
Below right: *Falafal are the staple snack of Israelis on the move.*

Food and Drink

A biblical law that 'a kid shall not seethe in its mother's milk' led to the rule that meat and milk should not be mixed. A kosher restaurant or home will keep two sets of crockery and utensils, one for milk and one for meat. Scavenging creatures like pigs and shellfish are considered unclean and are not eaten, although all sorts of crafty imitations do appear, like 'prawns' and crabsticks made of fish. Many Jews (Orthodox) will eat vegetarian food in a restaurant where the kosher observance is slightly suspect. Coming to terms with all the complexities of kosher and non-kosher takes a while but most visitors are amazed at the variety they find in Israeli cuisine: a breakfast buffet groaning under cheese platters and mounds of fruit or a candlelit feast of *chateaubriand* washed down with a very palatable red wine.

Many restaurants and most hotels observe kosher law, selling either meat or dairy products, but never both. A meat restaurant will serve margarine – not butter – non-dairy cream and no cheese sauces. Vegetarians will love the dairy restaurants, which are great for pasta, delicious cheeses, salad bars and creamy desserts. Most hotels have one outlet of each type.

'Typical' Israeli cuisine does not really exist. Like the people, Israeli food is a collection of cultures. If anything does typify eating in Israel, however, it's dishes

from the Middle East region, which include *falafal* – tiny balls of lentils, deep fried and stuffed into pitta bread – with salad; *hummous*, a garlicky chickpea dip; and smooth *tahini*, a paste made of sesame seeds. Kebabs of veal, chicken, lamb or beef are sold everywhere, usually with a vast salad. Try the *harit*, a spicy condiment that peps up the blandest *falafal*. Eastern European cooking, often regarded (wrongly) as 'typical' Jewish food, features in some homes: *gefilte* fish, chopped liver, borscht and Hungarian goulash.

Above: *For excellent dishes in a splendid setting, Jaffa's restaurants are hard to beat.*

Fish is sold everywhere. Grilled sardines are served on the beaches, and fishermen in Galilee still bring in plump, freshwater trout and the tasty St Peter fish, as they did in biblical times.

Of course, not all restaurants are kosher. An influx of Chinese, Vietnamese and Filipinos has led to the establishment of many Asian restaurants, with pork and prawns in abundance. Israel has its fair share of fast-food outlets, too, particularly in the big cities.

Fruit in Israel is magnificent and the markets have spectacular fruit displays. Kiwi, mango, pomegranate, passion fruit, custard apple and papaya are grown here, as are the world's largest strawberries and endless varieties of citrus.

Fruit juices from street vendors are wonderfully refreshing. Coffee is served black, strong and sweet (Turkish) or creamy and frothy (Viennese). *Botz* is the strong Israeli version of Turkish coffee.

Israelis are not big drinkers but the country produces some good wines (red and white) from the Carmel region, the Galilee and Rishon le-Zion, southeast of Tel Aviv. Local beers, bottled and draft, are available, and the local aniseed-flavoured firewater is called *arak*.

FESTIVAL NOSH

On Hannukah, small jelly doughnuts, or *sufganiot*, are eaten throughout Israel, as well as *latkes*, or potato pancakes. In January or February on Arbour Day, families eat fruit from biblical times such as olives, dates, pomegranates and figs. During Passover, everybody eats unleavened bread, in the form of small wafers which are made out of specially dry flour. The tradition stems from when Moses and the Israelites fled from Egypt – there was no time to leave the bread to rise, so they ate flat loaves. Tastier Passover fare includes coconut macaroons. If you dine with a Jewish family on Shabbat, expect *cholent*, a bean and meat stew that is baked on Friday.

2
Jerusalem

Exploring the walled **Old City** of Jerusalem is like peeling back layers of an onion; history unfolds as you descend from the bustling modern streets through time to the pillars and columns of the Roman era, 2000 years old, yet still standing under the buildings today.

Christians, Jews and Muslims have made Jerusalem their spiritual home and church bells ring as the haunting call to prayer echoes across rooftops from minarets. Visit the gold-domed mosque, the **Dome of the Rock**, or follow in Jesus' footsteps along the **Via Dolorosa** to the **Church of the Holy Sepulchre**, marking the spot of the crucifixion, burial and resurrection. Watch the devout praying at the **Western Wall**, the most sacred location for the Jewish faith.

Many faiths live in peace in war-ravaged Jerusalem, even sharing the same church in some cases. People are endlessly colourful, with sombre **Hassidic Jews**, chattering **Muslim Quarter** market stallholders, and awe-struck pilgrims soaking up the city's incredible atmosphere.

Jerusalem falls into three areas. The **Jewish West**, capital of Israel, is a busy, modern city and the seat of government (the Knesset). **East Jerusalem**, largely Arab, contains mosques, low-rise sandstone houses and fascinating biblical sites like the **Mount of Olives** and the **Garden of Gethsemane**. At the heart of Jerusalem is the walled **Old City** (parts of it are 3000 years old) which is a magnet to visitors from all over the world. Over $90 million was spent on renovating the city's unique attractions for the millennium celebrations in 2000.

DON'T MISS

★★★ Via Dolorosa: walk in the last footsteps of Jesus.
★★★ The Dome of the Rock: a spectacular mosque.
★★★ The Western Wall: the holiest site in the world for Jews.
★★ The Shrine of the Book: houses the Dead Sea Scrolls which are the oldest documents known to man.
★★ Arab Quarter: shopping heaven.
★★ The Church of the Holy Sepulchre: visit the heart of the Christian religion.

Opposite: *The magnificently tiled Dome of the Rock.*

Opposite top: *Jerusalem's fortified walls, studded with gates, encircle the city for over two miles.*

THE OLD CITY

Jerusalem's walled Old City is probably the most important site in Israel. The honey-coloured walls, which snake around the cluster of narrow streets and magnificent churches and temples for over two miles, are remarkably intact considering that they are over 400 years old. The Turkish ruler **Suleiman the Magnificent** was responsible for most of what remains today of the

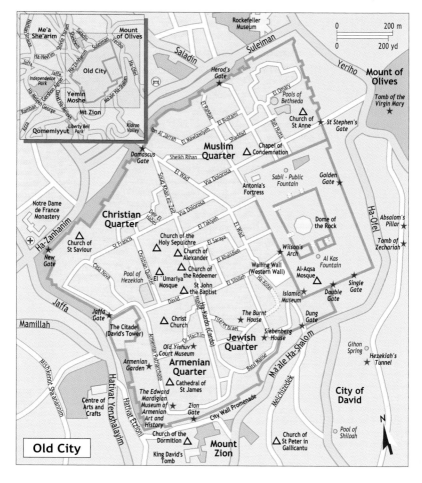

Old City

walls, constructed during 1538–41. Other parts date back to the **Crusaders**, and others even further back to **King Herod**. The walls, represent, literally, layer upon layer of history.

There are eight gates to the Old City, seven of which are open to people and cars. Belief has it that the eighth, the **Golden Gate** (sealed by the Muslims in the 7th century) will only open on Judgement Day. The gates are all known by their Arab, Jewish and English names. Moving clockwise along the northern wall, the first gate is the **Damascus Gate,** one of the most impressive Islamic buildings around. It is open from 09:00–16:00 Monday–Thursday, Saturday and Sunday; 09:00–14:00 Friday. About 100m (328ft) east is **Herod's Gate** where the Crusaders broke through the city walls in July 1099. It was mistakenly believed that Herod Antipas' palace was nearby, hence the gate's name.

St Stephen's Gate, named after the first Christian martyr who was stoned to death here, leads to the Mount of Olives and Gethsemane. The **Golden Gate** (the sealed entrance leading to the Temple Mount) is where, according to Christians, the Messiah will enter the city. The **Dung Gate**, the smallest of the gates, was so named because the area around this gate was once a rubbish dump! Parts of the **Zion Gate** had to be pulled down to give access to a Franciscan monastery that hadn't been incorporated within the city's walls.

The **Jaffa Gate** is important as it marked the point of arrival for people travelling from the ancient port of Jaffa. Lastly, the **New Gate** (opened in 1887) was built mainly to give access from the pilgrim hospices to the Christian holy sites of the Old City.

Below: *Jaffa Gate is a prominent entrance to the Old City.*

Opposite: *The Cardo was once the city's principal thoroughfare.*
Below: *The Armenian sector is a quiet, mysterious corner.*

The Tower of David ★★★

Located next to the **Jaffa Gate**, the most commonly used entrance for tourists, the Tower of David, or Citadel, was in fact built by Suleiman, not King David. The citadel stands on the site of a palace built by Herod the Great 2000 years ago, and the beautifully restored gardens in the centre contain relics from six different periods of Jerusalem's history.

Inside the Tower of David (which operates as the **Museum of the History of Jerusalem**), stone stairways lead from one display to the next, vividly telling the story of Jerusalem, with illuminated maps and models. Sound and light shows take place in the gardens in summer. Open 10:00–16:00 Sunday–Thursday; 10:00–14:00 Saturday; closed Fridays.

The Armenian Quarter ★★

A quiet quarter of the Old City, the Armenian sector has a hushed atmosphere, with priests in flowing black robes and grey beards moving noiselessly along the dark, narrow and ancient streets. Nestled under the wall to the right of the Tower of David, this area is nonetheless worth exploring for its tiny churches, ancient buildings and green, hidden courtyards.

Armenian Orthodox Monastery ★

Along the main alley, situated on the Armenian Patriarchate Road, is St James Cathedral. This church, built in honour of St James (who was beheaded on this site and became the first martyred disciple), is one of the oldest and most atmospheric churches in Jerusalem. Open 06:00–07:30, 15:00–15:30 daily.

The Edward Mardigian Museum of Armenian Art and History ★

On the same street, this art and history museum recounts the fascinating story of the Armenian community in Jerusalem through a collection of manuscripts and artefacts. Open 09:00–16:30 Monday– Saturday.

The Jewish Quarter ★★★

In the southeast corner of the city, bordered by the Armenian Quarter, the Western Wall and Hashalshelet Street, the Jewish Quarter's well-laid-out streets have been inhabited since the eighth century BC – but sadly destroyed many times. Today, the area is a peaceful oasis of smart shops, synagogues, street cafés and apartments, an ideal rest stop before plunging into the chaos of the Arab Quarter (*see* p. 39).

The Cardo ★★

Walk along the Cardo, a fascinating Roman street, laid down in the sixth century as the city's main thoroughfare. At various points, you can look down through glass sections at the ancient cobbled road and the remnants of arches and buildings from 1400 years ago.

Old Yishuv Court Museum ★

On Or Hachim Street, close to the Cardo, this museum depicts life in the **Jewish Quarter** from the 19th century to 1948. Walk around reconstructions of living quarters, kitchens and synagogues. Open 09:00–14:00 Monday–Thursday.

The Burnt House ★★

Would-be archaeologists should call in at the Burnt House on Tiferet Israel Street, where there's a fascinating audiovisual show of the excavations of the Jewish Quarter. This luxurious house belonged to a religious family in the **Second Temple Period** 538BC–AD70 (when the Jewish exiles returned from Babylon and rebuilt the

---

JEWISH ETIQUETTE

• Men and boys should wear a *kippa*, or skullcap, in a synagogue, at the Western Wall, at the Yad Vashem Holocaust Memorial, and at funerals. Normally, a *kippa* can be borrowed from the synagogue or site.

• Do not take photographs of the Western Wall on *Shabbat*; it is considered to be offensive.

• Modest dress is appropriate in religious places, particularly Me'a She'arim, where arms, legs and heads should not be exposed.

• In Tel Aviv's orthodox suburb of Brei Brak, no traffic is allowed on Shabbat and cars may be stoned.

• You can spend a Friday evening with an ultra-Orthodox family. Ask at tourist offices or at the Western Wall for information.

Above: Men and women pray separately at the Western Wall.

Temple) but was burnt in AD70 along with the rest of Jerusalem. Its sooty remains are better preserved than many of the other buildings and it has been converted into a museum. Open 09:00–17:00 Monday–Thursday and Saturday–Sunday; 09:00–13:00 Friday.

The Western Wall ★★★

Follow Tiferet Israel Street from the Burnt House to the stone steps leading down to the Western Wall, the most holy site of the Jewish people. The narrow streets open out into a wide plaza, often buzzing with tourists and worshippers. In front is the Wall, also known as the **Wailing Wall** or in Hebrew Ha-Kotel Ha-Ma'aravi (or the Kotel), and above it the **Temple Mount**, one-time location of the First and Second Temples. Today, the golden Dome of the Rock gleams above the wall in the sunlight. To the right, there's a warren of excavations – something in Jerusalem is always being dug up – leading to the walls and the **Dung Gate**. Visitors can explore the tunnels, via a new entrance in the Via Dolorosa.

The Western Wall itself is an imposing mass of carved stone blocks, 15m (50ft) tall and dating back 1900 years to King Herod's time. The wall is not part of the Temple itself, merely the support, but for Jews this is close enough. The 'Wailing' nickname comes from the fact that people come here to mourn the loss of their temple, first destroyed in 586BC by the Babylonians and again in AD70 by the Romans.

There are separate sections for men and women, and visitors must dress modestly to pray at the Wall. People write notes to God and push them between the ancient stones – this is supposed to make the wish come true. There's even a fax machine (courtesy of *Bezek*, the national phone company) so that people can send faxes to God. On **Shabbat**, there's a palpable atmosphere of reverence here as people rush to pray before sunset. Don't take photographs or smoke at this time.

Temple Mount ★★★

To Muslims, the holiest place in Jerusalem is the Temple Mount, reached via the stone staircase to the right of the Wailing Wall. The area is controlled by Jerusalem's Muslim authorities. Jews are forbidden from visiting the Mount by order of the chief Rabbinate – somewhere here is the final resting place of the Ark of the Covenant – only a High Priest is technically allowed to enter, and then only on Yom Kippur.

To the visitor, Temple Mount is a vast paved platform, surrounded by trees and bushes, looking down on the domed rooftops of the **Old City** in one direction and out over the scrub-covered **Mount of Olives** in the other. The First and Second Temples were built and destroyed here, and during the Islamic period the area became an important religious centre; **Mohammed** is believed to have ascended to heaven on his horse from here. Mosques were built but turned into churches by the **Crusaders**, and later, back into mosques. Also on the Temple Mount, according to the *Book of Matthew 4:5*, Satan took Jesus to the pinnacle of the temple to tempt him with the beautiful views.

A cautionary note: non-Muslims are only allowed to enter the Temple Mount through two gates, the **Gate of the Moors** and **Chain Gate**.

The Haram is free but you are required to pay to get into the two mosques and the museum. Opening hours are arranged around the Muslim prayer schedules but generally are as follows: 07:30–10:30, 12:30–13:30 (winter), 08:00–11:30, 13:30–15:00 (summer) Monday–Thursday, Saturday and Sunday. Closed on Friday. The Temple Mount is closed during Eid; during Ramadan it is open 07:30–10:00.

THE OLD CITY IN A DAY

With a car, it's possible to do a whistle-stop tour of the Old City and its surrounds. First, go through the Jaffa Gate to the Armenian Quarter, then use the Zion Gate which leads to the Jewish Quarter. Walk the Cardo, visit the Western Wall and the Temple Mount. Then walk the Via Dolorosa to the Holy Sepulchre. By car, visit the Garden Tomb, drive round the walls to the Garden of Gethsemane and up to the Mount of Olives to admire the view. Finish the tour at Absalom's Tomb at the top of the Kidron Valley.

Below: *Muslims outside the Dome of the Rock on Temple Mount.*

THE ART OF HAGGLING

Haggling is a way of life in the Arab *souqs* and visitors should be prepared to join in. Choose an item you like and decide what you think it is worth. The real value may be as little as one-fifth of the marked price. Politely make an offer and let the vendor express his horror. Accepting a cup of mint tea during the negotiations is all part of the process. Sometimes it pays to walk away; if the vendor comes running after you, you'll know he's likely to go lower. Being polite and friendly at all times pays.

Below: *Although the precise details of the construction of Al-Aqsa Mosque are a matter of dispute, the mosque can accommodate up to 5000 worshippers for prayer.*

The Dome of the Rock ★★★

This magnificent mosque, built between AD688–691, is the focal point of Jerusalem's skyline, its gold-plated aluminium dome appearing to light up the sky at sunset. The exterior is a myriad tiny, painted tiles in every imaginable shade of blue and green, topped by swirling inscriptions from the Koran. On Judgement Day, according to legend, the souls of mankind will be weighed on scales hung from the pillars at the top of the steps.

The mosque's ornate interior is taken up by a giant slab of rock, the Kubbet es-Sakhra. **Abraham** was said to have laid his son **Isaac** on this rock in preparation for sacrifice. **Mohammed** is supposed to have mounted his steed from it for his dream of flying to heaven. Beneath the rock, the spirits of the dead are believed to gather in a crypt, the **Well of Souls**. Some believe there is an abyss, not a crypt, in which the waters of the Flood roar eternally. Mohammed's footprints are supposed to be embedded on the rock, while Christians believe that it was here that Jesus discovered the written name of God.

Al-Aqsa Mosque ★★

The silver-topped Al-Aqsa Mosque at the southern end of the Mount, built over the massive underground caverns known as **Solomon's Stables**, is a vast prayer hall for 5000 people. It was destroyed and rebuilt several times; some believe it is a conversion of a Byzantine church, whilst Muslims believe it was built from scratch in the 8th century AD. In 1951 Jordan's King Abdullah was assassinated on the mosque's doorstep by a Muslim fanatic. It is open 08:30–11:00, 12:15–15:00, 16:00–17:00 Monday–Thursday and Saturday–Sunday. Closed on Friday.

The Arab Quarter ★★

After the open skies of the Temple Mount, take a deep breath and plunge into the chaotic sights, sounds and smells of the Arab Quarter. Two streets, **Souq Khan ez-Zeit** and **El Wad**, are traditional *souqs*, or markets, packed with trinkets, brass, Armenian tiles, Palestinian pottery, leather (often rather rancid and untreated), carvings and antiques. Some stalls sell huge piles of nuts; others are pungent with spices in brilliant reds and yellows. Sticky *baklava*, dripping with honey, and chunks of nougat are popular snacks. Carpets, clothing and gold-embroidered fabrics suspended over the narrow streets mean it's always dark in the *souq*; you'll be shouted at, pursued by enthusiastic stallholders and hassled from all angles. If you seriously intend buying anything, haggling is essential.

The Christian Quarter ★★★

The Christian Quarter occupies the northwest corner of the walled city, its focal point the **Church of the Holy Sepulchre**. In the maze of narrow but clean and orderly streets, the best and most popular route to follow is the **Via Dolorosa**, or the Way of the Cross, the route taken by Jesus from the **Praetorium** where he was condemned to death to **Calvary** where he was crucified. Groups of pilgrims move slowly along the narrow road, stopping to pray at each of the 14 stations (the stops Jesus made along the Via Dolorosa), many of them unable to believe that they are actually in Jerusalem, following Jesus' footsteps. The scene is incredibly moving. Somewhat less spiritual is the rampant commercialism that pervades the area, with the endless tacky souvenir shops and boutiques lining the route.

Via Dolorosa ★★★

Because Jerusalem has so many layers, the Via Dolorosa is unlikely to be the precise path that Jesus walked. The original is probably hidden under 2000 years of subsequent building. However, when the route and surrounding buildings were given a facelift, large slabs of stone were revealed along the way, believed to

Above: *View over the Arab Quarter of the Old City, with its fascinating market streets.*

JESUS CHRIST SUPERSTAR

The name Jesus is derived from a Greek version of the Hebrew name Joshua (or Yehoshuah, meaning 'Jehovah is deliverance'). The title 'Christ' comes from the Greek word, Christos, a translation of the Hebrew, Mashiakh or Messiah. 'Christ' was used by Jesus' early followers, who regarded him as the promised deliverer of Israel and later it was included as part of Jesus' proper name by the church, which regards him as the redeemer of all humanity.

HOLY TEACHINGS

The bibles of Judaism and Christianity are different. The Jewish Bible consists of the Old Testament, 39 books originally written in Hebrew, except for a few sections which are written in Aramaic (the ancient language of the Middle East). The Christian Bible is comprised of two parts: the Old Testament and the 27 Books of the New Testament (originally written in Greek). The Old Testament is structured in two slightly different forms by Catholics and Protestants. Roman Catholics use the Jewish Bible plus seven other books and additions; Protestants limit it to the 39 books of the Jewish Bible.

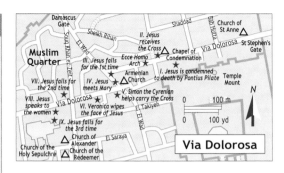

Via Dolorosa

date back to Roman times. The route begins in the Arab Quarter, just inside **St Stephen's Gate** and the 'Stations of the Cross' are illuminated for night-time visitors. Guided tours operate daily from the Pilgrim's Reception Plaza opposite the **Crusader Church of St Anne**, which marks Mary's birthplace, and the **Pool of Bethseda**, where Jesus healed the cripple.

The **First Station of the Cross**, where Pilate sentenced Jesus to death, is in the courtyard of the **Umariyah School**. The actual setting is believed to have been Herod's Antonia Fortress, the foundations now covered by the churches lining the Via Dolorosa. The **Ecce Homo Arch** outside the Church of the Sisters of Zion takes its name from Pilate's sneer at Jesus, 'Behold the man'.

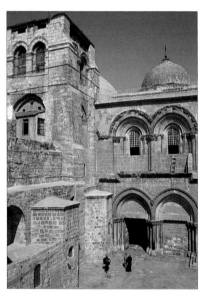

The **Second Station**, where Jesus received his cross and had a crown of thorns placed on his head, is opposite the Franciscan Church of the Condemnation. The **Third**, which marks his first fall, is at the point where Via Dolorosa crosses the street El Wad. The **Fourth Station**, where Jesus met his mother, Mary, is marked by an Armenian Church. At the **Fifth Station**, Simon the Cyrenian helped Jesus carry the cross. The House of St Veronica marks the **Sixth**, where Veronica wiped Jesus' face with her veil.

The Via Dolorosa then bisects the *souq* Kahn ez-Zeit, the location of the **Seventh Station**, where Jesus fell for the second time. Two more stations lie outside the Church of the Holy Sepulchre. The **Eighth** is marked by a Greek Orthodox chapel, St Charalambous, built over the spot where Jesus spoke to the women of Jerusalem: 'Weep not for me, but for Jerusalem.' A pillar marks the point at which he fell a third time – the **Ninth Station**. The remaining five stations are contained within the Church of the Holy Sepulchre.

Church of the Holy Sepulchre ★★★

The squat Church of the Holy Sepulchre, the heart of the Christian Quarter, covers **Calvary** (**Golgotha** in Hebrew), the Place of the Skull. Much of the present structure dates from the 12th century, built by the Crusaders, although a place of worship has stood here since the 4th century.

The Holy Sepulchre is actually a cluster of five churches, some with a bigger part of the communal space than others. For visitors, it's difficult to distinguish between Armenian and Greek Orthodox, Syrian Orthodox, Roman Catholic and Abyssinian Coptic, and there's always a service going on somewhere in the maze, chanting in different languages, the air heavy with incense and bearded priests scuttling backwards and forwards in the dim light. Hapless tourists are bound to shuffle around the remaining five stations in slow-moving lines. To grasp the significance of each area, enlisting a professional guide is a good idea.

Inside the door, up a flight of steps, is Golgotha and the **10th Station**, where Jesus was stripped. A mosaic in the floor tells the story. The next three stations, located close together and marked by altars, attract large crowds. Here Jesus was nailed to the Cross, the Cross was hoisted upright, and his body was later taken down. The final, **14th Station** is the Holy Sepulchre itself. The marble tomb below contains the rock that guarded the entrance, the burial site, and the tomb of **Joseph of Arimathea**. Open 05:30–21:00 April–September daily; 04:30–19:00 October–March daily.

Above: *Ethiopian Coptic bell-ringer in the Church of the Holy Sepulchre.*
Opposite: *The Holy Sepulchre is home to five religions in all.*

MESSENGERS OF GOD

'Apostle' derives from the Greek for 'messenger'. Historians believe that Jesus may have chosen twelve apostles, or disciples, to represent symbolically the Twelve Tribes of Israel. The twelve were Peter the fisherman, Andrew, James the Great, John, Philip, Bartholomew, Thomas, Matthew, James the Less, Thaddaeus, Simon the Canaanite, and Judas Iscariot, who would later betray Jesus. Matthias was chosen in place of Judas. In the early church the title 'apostle' was extended to others who spread the Christian message, such as Paul, Barnabas, and Timothy.

EAST JERUSALEM
The Garden Tomb ★

Anglicans believe that the 'real' Golgotha lies outside the
current city walls. The **Garden Tomb**, through the
Damascus Gate, does match the biblical description.
The hill beside it is shaped like a skull and the rock-
hewn cavern is typical of the time. The tomb was
discovered in 1883 by General Charles Gordon. Today,
it is maintained by the **British Garden Tomb Association**,
the entrance overlooking an English country garden.
Open April–September 08:00–12:00, 14:30–18:00 daily;
October–March 08:00–12:00, 14:30–17:00 daily.

Rockefeller Museum ★★

Close by, the Rockefeller Museum houses an interesting
display of archaeological finds, including human bones
from the Carmel area, dating back 100,000 years.
Open 10:00–15:00 Sunday–Thursday, 10:00–14:00
Saturday, closed Friday.

Solomon's Quarries ★★

Also worth a visit on this side of the city is a mysterious underground cave system, situated between Herod's and Damascus' Gates. Probably a quarry, this could have been the source of stone for Solomon's temple. Some people believe that the caves lead all the way to Jericho; King Zedekiah was supposed to have fled from the Babylonians through the caves in 587BC and is said to have been captured somewhere near Jericho. You can explore the caves 09:00–16:00, Monday–Thursday and Saturday; 09:00–14:00 Fridays.

The Mount of Olives ★★★

The Mount of Olives, rising up behind the Old City in East Jerusalem, is the best place to go for spectacular views. Sunrise and sunset are the most beautiful times.

The olive-less hill is steeped in legend and belief. The Jewish cemetery, still in use, dates back to biblical times and is considered the most sacred in the world. Jesus is believed to have entered Jerusalem from the Mount of Olives, through the **Golden Gate**, now sealed until the arrival of the next Messiah. Jews and Christians believe that a second Messiah will resurrect the dead and lead them once again through the gate, so the Mount of Olives is in great demand as a burial site. The most unlikely people have chosen this as their final resting place, including publisher Robert Maxwell. Also buried here is Oskar Schindler, one of the Germans who helped Jews in World War II, and whose story was later made into the award-winning film *Schindler's List*.

There are several interesting churches on the Mount of Olives. The **Dome of the Ascension**, now a mosque, marks the spot from which Jesus is believed to have ascended to Heaven. On the path that leads down to the city, the walls of the **Pater Noster Carmelite Convent** are decorated with the Lord's Prayer.

Above: *The cemetery on the Mount of Olives is much in demand.*
Opposite: *Jerusalem stretches out below the Mount of Olives, with the Old City in the middle ground and, beyond, high-rise buildings of the modern city.*

Above: *A number of Israel's gnarled olive trees, seen here in the Garden of Gethsemane, are believed to date back to the time of Jesus.*

Garden of Gethsemane ★

Next to the **Church of All Nations**, at the foot of the hill is the Garden of Gethsemane, where Jesus was betrayed and arrested. The gnarled olive trees in the garden are believed to be around 2000 years old and it may well have been from one of these that the disciple, Judas, hanged himself. It is open 08:00–12:00, 13:00–16:00 daily.

Mary's Tomb ★

A path to the left of the garden leads underground to the candlelit tombs of the Virgin Mary's parents, Anne and Joachim. The 5th-century chapel also contains the remains of Mary herself and her husband, Joseph. Open 06:00–11:45, 14:30–17:00 daily.

The Kidron Valley ★★

Outside the Dung Gate of the Old City is a fascinating archaeological dig, slowly uncovering the **City of David** on the slopes of the Kidron Valley. Before the First Temple was built, the city was located here on **Mount Ophel**, mainly because of the Gihon Spring which emerges at the foot of the hill. The spring is connected to the **Siloam Pool**, 500m (550yd) down the valley, by **Hezekiah's Tunnel**, an amazing feat of ancient engineering. Visitors can trudge through the wet tunnel, holding a lantern, a walk that takes about 40 minutes. Open 08:30–15:00 Monday–Thursday, Saturday–Sunday; 09:30–13:00 Friday.

There are three impressive tombs in the Kidron Valley, too. The **Pillar of Absalom** and the **Tomb of Zechariah** are fascinating examples of 3000-year-old architecture, with graceful pillars and friezes. The third monument, the **Tomb of Hezir**, is part of the same necropolis.

HEZEKIAH'S TUNNEL

In 701 BC, Hezekiah, King of Judah, designed an ingenious tunnel connecting the **Gihon Spring**, the city's only water supply outside the city, to within the walls, creating the **Siloam Pool** to avoid having the water source cut off by the enemy. Workmen dug from both ends, zigzagging under the city until they met in the middle. In the 19th century, archaeologist Charles Warren even discovered a secret shaft, reaching up to an underground passage where the residents could come to draw water, now known as **Warren's Shaft**.

MOUNT ZION ★★

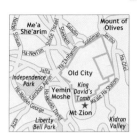

Mount Zion, a rounded hillock outside the **Zion Gate**, appears as something rather more substantial in the Bible. It was here that the Virgin Mary is said to have died, a spot now marked by the **Dormition Abbey**. Jesus is also said to have washed the disciples' feet here before the **Last Supper**.

Symbolic with the promise of a Jewish homeland, Mount Zion has also been the subject of political tussles over the years. Suleiman is supposed to have executed the architect who designed the city walls here for failing to include Mount Zion in what was then Jerusalem.

King David's Tomb ★

Unlikely to be the real tomb of King David, this rock tomb is nevertheless part of the tourist trail. Open 08:00–18:00 Saturday–Thursday, until 14:00 on Fridays.

Chamber of the Holocaust ★

In a cellar next to the tomb, this small, candlelit museum is dedicated to the six million victims of the Holocaust. Open 08:00–18:00 Sunday–Thursday, until 15:00 on Fridays.

Below: *Walking is easily the best way to explore the several fascinating tombs located outside the city walls.*

PLACE NAMES

The variety of names for each place is hardly surprising, given the number of different factions that have settled in Israel over time.
- **Jerusalem** is also **Yerushalayim** (Israeli) and **al-Quads ash-sharif** (Muslim).
- **Jaffa** is also **Joppa** and **Yafo**.
- **Eilat** is also **Elath** and **Elat**.
- **Acre** may appear as **Acco** and **Akko**.
- **Lake Tiberias** is the same as **Lake Kinneret** (Israeli) and the **Sea of Galilee** (Christian).

Below: *Among the city's plushest hotels is the King David.*

WEST JERUSALEM

The 'new' Jerusalem is a lively modern city, surprisingly green with tall cypress and shady pine trees. The shops and restaurants of **Zion Square** are a good place to get your bearings and enjoy a cool fruit juice. Just off the square, **Ben Yehuda** and **Yoel Salomon** streets are pretty pedestrianized areas with plenty of art and craft shops.

King David Hotel ★

Located on Ha-Melekh David Street, this hotel is a Jerusalem landmark. The British used it as a base during the Mandate Period and a whole wing was blown up in July 1946 by the Jewish Underground, who hid bombs in milk churns. Bomb warnings were ignored and 91 people died, leading for calls for the British to withdraw from Israel. This event did not deter modern heads of state, all of whom stay here today.

Herod's Family Tomb ★

In the park behind the hotel is the family tomb of the egotistical King Herod, where he allegedly buried his wife Mariamne and his two sons, after murdering them in a jealous rage. Open 10:00–13:00 Monday–Thursday.

Opposite the King David Hotel, the **YMCA** is another celebrated building. It was designed in 1928–33 by architects Shreve, Lamb and Harmon, who were also responsible for the Empire State Building in New York City. Not unlike the graceful minaret of a mosque, the 35m (120-foot) tower offers stunning views of the city.

Yemin Moshe ★★

The most desirable address in Jerusalem today is Yemin Moshe, overlooking the Old City and topped by a stone windmill. Its pretty stone buildings were the homes of the first Jewish colony to settle outside the safety of the city walls.

The patron of the colony, the English-Jewish philanthropist **Sir Moses Montefiore**, visited Jerusalem in 1858 and was so appalled by the cramped conditions within the walls that he decided to sponsor a new suburb. He enlisted wealthy New Orleans Jew, **Judah Touro**, to help with the ambitious project.

The new town was called **Mishkenot Sha'ananim**, or 'peaceful dwellings', and later renamed **Yemin Moshe**. It was badly damaged in the 1967 war but was rebuilt and soon established itself as a fashionable, artistic neighbourhood. The windmill at the top was a working structure, providing flour for the colony. In 1948 it served as an important observation post for

the Israeli army. Now it's a small museum depicting the life of Montefiore. Open 09:00–16:00 Sunday–Thursday, 09:00–13:00 Friday.

Above: *The striking YMCA has a fine restaurant.*

Me'a She'arim ★

A few blocks north of Zion Square is the fascinating shtetl (East European-style Orthodox ghetto) of **Me'a She'arim**, built in 1875 as a refuge for the ultra-Orthodox **Hassidim**. Walking through the narrow streets is like stepping back in time; old synagogues and grey buildings line the narrow streets, and the devout residents, all pale-faced and bespectacled, sport black hats, long black robes and strange, curly sidelocks of hair. Visitors are welcome but respectful dress and behaviour must be taken very seriously.

BAR FLIES

Jerusalem has plenty of lively places in which to spend the evening. Coffee bars along Ben Yehuda Street are always busy, and Aroma on Hilel Street is very popular with young people. Around the Russian Compound are several bars with music, most getting busy around midnight. The rather dubiously named Kanabis is fashionable.

Above: *Poignant sculpture at the Yad Vashem memorial.*

Israel Museum ★★★★

The spectacular Israel Museum, the largest in Israel, is an essential stop on a tour of Jerusalem. The museum covers art, archaeology, ethnology and its highlight, the **Dead Sea Scrolls**.

The Dead Sea Scrolls, the oldest surviving biblical texts in the world, are housed in the **Shrine of the Book**, a dazzling white dome. The Shrine has been shaped to represent the lid of the jars in which the scrolls were found.

The scrolls themselves, fragile scraps of parchment beautifully laid out under glass, are awe-inspiring. To understand more about the times of the Old Testament, visit the breathtaking archaeological section where 6000-year-old pottery figures, Canaanite sarcophagi and 4000-year-old metalwork are housed, alongside tomb inscriptions dating from the time of Jesus.

The art sections are equally well laid out, if less dramatic, with sections of Jewish art, some good Impressionist work including Renoirs and Van Goghs, and outside, the attractive **Billy Rose Sculpture Gardens**. Wild herbs grow amongst the orderly flowerbeds and sculptures and there are magnificent views of the city. Open 10:00–17:00 Monday, Wednesday, Thursday, Sunday; 16:00–22:00 Tuesday and 10:00–14:00 Friday.

Yad Vashem Memorial ★★

Some distance further west on **Mount Herzl** is the poignant **Holocaust Memorial**, dedicated to the six million Jews who were murdered by the Nazis. The main room, the **Hall of Remembrance**, has a mosaic floor inscribed with the names of the 22 largest death camps, among them **Dachau** and **Auschwitz**. Ashes of the victims are kept in an underground vault and an eternal flame burns. In the children's section, mirrors create a

---

SAMSON'S BETRAYAL

Old Testament hero, Samson, was endowed by God with supernatural strength, provided no no razor touched his long locks. Samson performed several great feats, including the strangling of a lion and the slaying of a thousand Philistines with the jaw bone of an ass. Then he was betrayed by his Philistine lover, Delilah, who had his head shaved and thereafter handed him over to the Philistines. He was blinded and made a slave. But according to the *Book of Judges*, when Samson's hair grew back, he was once again able to exert his great strength at a Philistine festival where he was being paraded. He pulled down the pillars of the house in which 3000 Philistines had assembled, burying the mob and himself in the ruins.

point of light for every one of the one-and-a-half million children who died in the Holocaust, while the **Valley of Destroyed Communities** is a huge map of Europe, marking the 5000 communities that were lost forever.

There's also an art section, displaying work by the inmates of the camps and five sculptures in the grounds outside. The **Avenue of Righteous Gentiles**, leading up to the main building, contains rows of trees planted in honour of gentiles who risked their lives to help Jews during World War II. Open 09:00–16:45 Monday–Thursday, Sunday; 09:00–13:45 Friday.

Herzl Museum ★

On the same hill is the museum dedicated to **Theodor Herzl**, the Viennese lawyer and writer credited with the foundation of Zionism. His black granite tomb marks the hilltop outside.

Above left and below:
The Shrine of the Book resembles the lid of pots that contained the Dead Sea Scrolls.

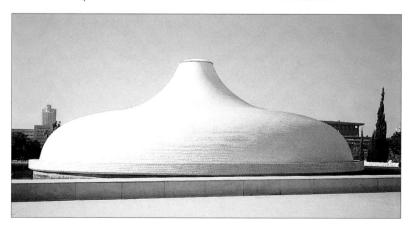

Jerusalem at a Glance

Best Times to Visit

March to May and late **September to October** are the best times to visit as the heat is not too oppressive. Winter in Jerusalem can be damp, grey and chilly (or dazzlingly clear), so take warm clothes for November to February. Midsummer can be very hot, which makes sightseeing more difficult. **September** is the main Jewish holiday period, so check the calendar before planning a trip as many attractions will be closed at this time.

Getting There

The gateway airport for Jerusalem is Tel Aviv's **Ben-Gurion International Airport**, served by flights from all over the world. Jerusalem is about 40 minutes' drive by taxi, slightly more by **Egged** bus, tel: toll free (177) 022-5555. Buses run from Sunday to midnight on Friday and are cheap. Trains run regularly from Tel Aviv central station, tel: (03) 542-1515, to Jerusalem, tel: (02) 673-3764 (but not from the airport). Car rental companies also have offices at the airport. Coming by road from Jordan, the Allenby Bridge is the closest border point.

Getting Around

Walking is the most pleasant way to get around Jerusalem's Old City and there are plenty of guided tours. Otherwise,

buses run all over the city from Jaffa Road and Zion Square; Egged information, tel: (03) 694-8888. **Taxis** can be booked by telephone or hailed on the street and *sherut* (shared taxis), which must be booked in advance, depart from Zion Square. Jerusalem has a small domestic airport, Atarot, served by the domestic carrier **Arkia**, tel: (02) 625-5888.

Where to Stay

Jerusalem offers the complete range of accommodation, from five-star deluxe hotels to simple hostels, youth hostels, Christian or Jewish hostels and even a kibbutz within the city limits. Most of the hotels have kosher restaurants. Note: if you pay in dollars rather than shekels, you will avoid the 17% VAT.

Luxury
King David, 23 Ha-Melekh David, Jerusalem, tel: (02) 620-8888, fax: (02) 620-8880. Israel's grandest hotel, with beautiful gardens and sumptuous decor, and visited by politicians and celebrities.
American Colony Hotel, Nablus Road, Jerusalem, tel: (02) 627-9777, e-mail: reserv@amcol.co.il Beautiful, atmospheric hotel built in an old pasha's palace, set in leafy grounds.
Crowne Plaza, Givat Ram, Jerusalem, tel: (02) 658-8888,

e-mail: res@hill.co.il Large, modern tower with all amenities and great views over the city.

Mid-Range
Palace Hotel, Mount of Olives, Jerusalem, tel: (02) 627-1125. Good location for Old City visits. All rooms have a private bathroom.
Jerusalem Tower Hotel, 23 Rehov Hillel, tel: (02) 620-9209, e-mail: towerjerusalem@isrotel.co.il Comfortable three-star hotel in the centre of the New City. All rooms with private bathroom.
Novotel, 9 St George Street, tel: (02) 532-0000, fax: (02) 532-7241. Modern chain hotel with restaurant.

Budget
YMCA Three Arches, 26 Ha-Melekh David, tel: (02) 569-2692, fax: (02) 623-5192. Landmark building in the city centre with superb views from the bell tower and pleasant rooms.
Louise Waterman-Wise, 8 Rehov Hapisga, Bayit Vegan, tel: (02) 642-3366, fax: (02) 642-3362. Pleasant hostel near the Israel Museum.
Ramat Rachel, Kibbutz Ramat Rachel, Jerusalem, tel: (02) 670-2555, www.ramatrachel.co.il

A modern kibbutz within the city boundaries of Jerusalem, overlooking the desert, including a swimming pool and fitness centre.

WHERE TO EAT

Jerusalem is a great city for coffee bars and street dining, from the Arab stalls in the Old City to the pavement cafés along Ben Yehuda. Explore everything from Middle Eastern specialities (known as Oriental) to French gourmet, Italian and Asian.

LUXURY
American Colony Hotel, Nablus Road, tel: (02) 627-9777. Quiet, elegant surroundings. Barbecues are held in the garden on Saturdays in summer. **Ocean**, 7 Rivlin, Jerusalem, tel: (02) 624-7501. Reputed to be the best fish restaurant in Israel.

MID-RANGE
Cardo Culinarium, Cardo, Jewish Quarter, Old City, tel: (02) 626-4155. Roman banquet using only ingredients available in biblical times. **Yemenite Step Kosher Restaurant**, 10 Yoel Solomon Street, New City, tel: (02) 624-0477. Jerusalem's oldest Yemenite restaurant. **Le Tsriff**, YMCA Hotel, tel: (02) 623-1154. Terrace dining at the spectacular YMCA building. French and vegetarian food, huge baked pies.

BUDGET
Off the Square, 6 Yoel Salomon Street, New City, tel: (02) 566-5956. Two restaurants in one, dairy and meat, with dairy section built around a patio. Kosher.

SHOPPING

Jerusalem has several excellent and contrasting shopping areas. In the Old City, the **Cardo** is lined with all of the designer stores, while the **Arab Quarter** is exactly the opposite – lively, smelly, colourful and noisy, with trinkets hanging in all the doorways and where haggling is mandatory. There are also several shopping malls, the best of which is **Ben Yehuda** in the New City, which is packed with restaurants and cafés. Religious souvenirs can be bought in **Me'a She'arim**.

TOURS AND EXCURSIONS

All the main tour companies are based in Jerusalem and Tel Aviv and there are countless excursions to choose from, by air-conditioned coach, minibus or private taxi. Day trips include Bethlehem; Tel Aviv and Jaffa; Masada and the Dead Sea; Galilee and the Golan Heights; Tiberias, Akko and Caesarea; and Eilat. The biggest tour operator is **Egged**, tel: (03) 694-8888. **Metzoke Dragot**, tel: (02) 994-4222, arranges trips into the Judean Desert from Jerusalem. For tours around Jerusalem, take the Line 99 double-decker bus, which operates Sun–Fri and has 27 stops. A ticket allows you to get on and off as you please. Commentary in several languages; tel: (03) 694-8888.

USEFUL CONTACTS

Tower of David Museum, tel: (02) 626-5333. **Tourist information**, Safra Square, tel: (02) 625-8844, or Jaffa Gate, tel: (02) 628-0382. **Christian Information Centre**, Jaffa Gate, tel: (02) 627-2692. **Israel Antiquities Authority**, POB 586, Jerusalem, tel: (02) 620-4693, for information on joining a dig. **El Al**, tel: (03) 971-6111 or (03) 971-6281. **Car rental**: Thrifty, 8 King David Street, tel: 1-800-377777.

JERUSALEM	J	F	M	A	M	J	J	A	S	O	N	D
AVERAGE TEMP. °F	48	48	55	61	68	73	75	77	73	70	61	52
AVERAGE TEMP. °C	9	9	13	16	20	23	24	25	23	21	16	11
Hours of sun daily	6	7	7	10	11	14	13	13	11	7	7	6
RAINFALL in	5.2	5.2	2.5	1.09	.11	0	0	0	0	.51	2.8	3.4
RAINFALL mm	132	132	64	28	3	0	0	0	0	13	71	86
Days of rainfall	18	18	12	5	2	0	0	0	0	3	12	14

3
The West Bank

The West Bank is one of Israel's most 'biblical' land-scapes: low, rolling hills dotted with dusty olive trees, grazing donkeys and goats, rocky terraces, Bedouin encampments, and grubby children playing in the dust. From the hills outside Jerusalem, it is easy to spot the distant blue, metallic glint of the Dead Sea. Somewhat less biblical is the Arabic graffiti scrawled over every building. This is one of the most politically tense areas of the Middle East and travel in this region can have an edge to it.

'West Bank' refers to the bank of the **River Jordan**, which divides Israel from its neighbour. Jordan annexed the region in 1950 and Israel subsequently gained control of it in 1967 during the Six-Day War. The area is important for Israel; without this strip of land, there would be just 15km (9½ miles) between Jordan and the Mediterranean in places, making Israeli territory dangerously thin. Several areas in the West Bank have since been handed back to the Palestinians, among them the towns of Nablus, Ramallah, Tulkarm, Jenin, Bethlehem and Jericho.

Many fascinating biblical sights are located on the West Bank. They are not always safe to visit, so staying abreast of the political situation is part of everyday life here. Travel alone or travel at night are not recommended. **Bethlehem**, birthplace of Jesus, and **Jericho**, the oldest city known to man, are popular. Southeast of Bethlehem is **Herodian**, King Herod's magnificant desert citadel, and the grand monastery of **Mar Saba**.

DON'T MISS

*** The Church of the Nativity: one of the world's oldest working churches.
*** Jericho: oldest city in the world.
** Herodian: King Herod's spectacular desert fortress.
** Sebastya: view its impressive Roman remains.
** Wadi Qelt: experience its beautiful hiking scenery with pools along the way.

Opposite: *Rural transport on the road to Jericho.*

North of Jerusalem are several spots of biblical significance – **Beit El**, where Jacob dreamed of a ladder ascending to Heaven, and **Shiloh**, where the Ark of the Covenant was once housed.

BETHLEHEM

Below: *Although other details of his life are occasionally subject to dispute, it is agreed that Jesus was born in Bethlehem; the Church of the Nativity has long been an essential religious site.*

Bethlehem is only 11km (7 miles) south of Jerusalem but the difference in scenery is vivid: buildings are run-down and scruffy, people wear Arab head-dresses, and graffiti covers every crumbling wall. Cars here even have blue licence plates. It's almost like being in another country! This unassuming little town is nonetheless a religious hotspot and to many visitors, the **Church of the Nativity** is as essential a site as the Holy Sepulchre is in the city of Jerusalem.

Church of the Nativity ★★

A solid-looking structure on **Manger Square** (today a parking lot surrounded by cheap souvenir stalls), the Church of the Nativity, or at least its original basilica, has stood here since AD325, and was built by the Emperor Constantine. Emperor Justinian later rebuilt it in the 6th century. Like the Church of the Holy Sepulchre in Jerusalem, the Church of the Nativity is too important a spot for only one denomination to occupy and there are Greek Orthodox, Armenian and Franciscan sections in this place of worship.

The door, bricked up by the Crusaders to stop enemies charging in on horseback, is so low you have to stoop to get in. Inside, in the sombre gloom,

gold-coloured lamps hang from the thick wooden ceiling and parts of the wooden floor gape open, revealing the old mosaics underneath.

The tiny **Grotto of the Nativity** is down some rather dark stone steps, a faded mosaic on the altar and a silver star on the floor marking the spot where Jesus was born. At times, the grotto can get very crowded. Next door, the **Chapel of the Manger** is where Mary placed the baby Jesus in a manger – the reality, experts agree, is that Jesus was born not in a stable but in a cave or grotto similar to this; many houses in Bethlehem are still built backing onto the hill, which is riddled with caves. The actual manger is now kept in Rome in the Church of Santa Maria Maggiore. Open 06:00–18:00 daily.

Milk Grotto ★

Along Milk Grotto Street, which leads off Manger Square, is a limestone cave of important religious significance. Legend has it that while Mary and Joseph were preparing to flee Bethlehem, some of Mary's milk splashed on the floor as she was nursing the baby, whitening the red rock. Nowadays Christians and

Above: *A silver star marks the spot where Jesus was born.*

JOSEPH, INTERPRETER OF DREAMS

Favourite son of Jacob, Joseph was envied by his 11 brothers, who sold him as a slave to a pharoah. Joseph, however, could interpret dreams and won the favour of the pharaoh by prophesying seven years of feast followed by seven years of famine. The pharaoh made Joseph his highest official and charged him with collecting food to be used during the years of famine. When the famine arrived, the Egyptians were able to survive as a result. The brothers came to Egypt, begging for food, and the family was reconciled.

Above: *Franciscan monks eke out a living from the land near Bethlehem.*

Muslims believe that a visit to the cave will increase fertility and promote better breast-feeding. Visitors have been chipping away at the white stone for years. Little packets are sold by the souvenir vendors.

The Shepherds' Fields ★

A visit to Bethlehem would not be complete without looking at the fields where shepherds watched their flocks and saw the angels proclaiming the birth of Christ. Visit the fields by taxi or by walking the short distance along the imaginatively named Shepherd's Street off Manger Square to the Arab village of **Beit Salur**. Two churches mark the spot where the shepherds were supposedly sitting: a Greek church stands in the field, while the **Franciscan Church of the Angels** covers the caves where the shepherds lived.

King David's Well ★

Also in Bethlehem is David's Well, consisting of three rock-hewn water cisterns, situated on Manger Street opposite the King David Cinema. During a battle with the Philistines, King David sent three of his men to break through the Philistine ranks to fetch water. But when they returned, the king sacrificed the water to God, rather than 'drink the blood of the men who went at the risk of their lives'.

AROUND BETHLEHEM
The Tomb of Rachel ★

Just outside Bethlehem, at the intersection of Hebron Road and Manger Street (a 30-minute walk from Manger Square), is the burial place of Rachel, mother of Benjamin and wife of Jacob. Jews, Muslims and Christians worship here at a simple structure built in the 19th century by the British Jew and philanthropist, **Sir Moses Montefiore**. Open 08:00–17:00 (18:00 in summer) Monday–Thursday, Sunday; 08:00–13:00 Friday; closed on Saturday.

Solomon's Pools ★★

Some 4km (2½ miles) from Bethlehem, heading south, are Solomon's Pools, three murky, green cisterns dating back to Roman times (though some sources date them to the time of King Solomon, the 10th century BC). There is some contention over when they were built, but the pools are nevertheless a remarkable feat of engineering and acted as an important source of water for Jerusalem. Partly supplied by rainwater and partly by springs, the pools were tapped by an aqueduct which worked with

WEST BANK DO'S AND DON'TS

- Do check the political climate before visiting the West Bank.
- Do dress modestly.
- Do dress like a tourist, for once! If you don't look Arabic or Israeli, you should be left alone.
- Do travel on a tour bus, less likely to be a target for *Intifada* protestors.
- Don't take a car with Israeli plates into the Palestinian-controlled cities. Use the bypass instead.
- Don't expect to spend the night.
- Do talk to the Palestinians; they're friendly and hospitable.

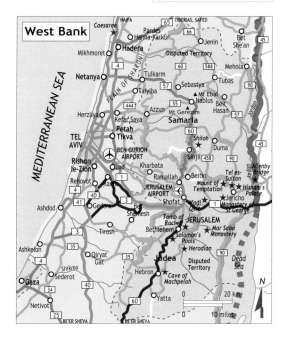

gravity, sloping down towards Jerusalem's Temple Mount. A later aqueduct worked by siphon and flowed via Bethlehem to Jerusalem. The system continued to work until 1947, although Jerusalem now gets its water supply from the Sea of Galilee.

Above: *Solomon's Pools were the main water supply for Jerusalem until the 1940s.*

Herodian ★★★

Moving up from the desert plains, Herodium, as it was once known, is a vast monument to the ego of **Herod the Great**. This impenetrable fortress palace was built by the king between 24–15BC, firstly to commemorate the spot where he won a battle; secondly as a retreat for himself and his cronies; and thirdly as a refuge, in the event that there wouldn't be enough time to reach Masada, his other 'bolt hole' on the Dead Sea. Open 08:00–17:00 Monday–Thursday, Saturday; 08:00–16:00 Friday.

Herodian was a small town in its day, containing hot baths, banqueting halls, a synagogue, and four watchtowers inside its 100-metre-high walls. After Herod's death in AD4, Herodian became the **king's mausoleum**.

Below: *Little remains of Herod's great fortress in the desert.*

Zealots captured it in AD66, but were defeated by the **Romans** in AD130. After a second defeat by the Romans, the only occupants left were monks, who lived in cells and built a chapel for their worship. Crusaders camped here temporarily after the monks had been driven out by the Romans, but for the 1300 years since, Herodian has been uninhabited and, not

surprisingly, is crumbling badly. There are plenty of ruined parts to see and the view from the top is breathtaking. Views encompass the skyline of Jerusalem to the north, the shimmering Dead Sea to the southeast and mile upon mile of Judean Desert to the west.

Above: *The mausoleum of Herodian is a lonely place today.*

Mar Saba Monastery ★★
Clinging to a cliff face overlooking the gorge of the **Kidron River**, this 5th-century Greek Orthodox monastery is a worthwhile diversion a few miles east of Bethlehem. The monastery was built in AD492 by St Sabas, who had previously favoured this beautiful desert retreat for contemplation. Some 5000 monks lived here once, mostly in natural caves in the hillside. Marauding Arabs and Persians killed all the monks in the seventh century and the victims' skulls are displayed inside the monastery, as are the remains of St Sabas himself, donated to Israel by Italy in 1965.

During the eighth century, **John of Damascus** came here to write. However, Mar Saba continued to suffer regular sackings until 1840, when it was rebuilt using funds from the Russian government.

A fortress-like wall surrounds the monastery, making it seem part of the cliff face. Only men are allowed inside and only if they are modestly clad. Women must be content with the view from the tower into the monastery.

SHIP OF THE DESERT

The camel is well adapted to its surroundings. The Arabian camel eats the thorny plants that grow in the desert and stores fat in its hump. It can survive for days without water. Thick, broad pads on its soles and calluses on the knees and chest, upon which the camel rests in a kneeling position, enable it to withstand the heat of the sand. The camel can close its nostrils against flying dust and its eyes are shielded by very long eyelashes. It can also cover more than 161km (100 miles) in a day. The flesh and milk of the camel can be used as food, and the hide for leather, while the long hair, which is shed every summer, is made into fine brushes and camel-hair cloth.

Below: *Abraham's tomb in Hebron is the cause of much controversy.*

HEBRON

Some 16km (10 miles) south of Bethlehem lies another political hot spot, the ancient town of Hebron. Hebron is distinctively Arabic, complete with a labyrinthine *souq*, the babble of Arab voices, noisy market trading, mosques and a major Islamic university.

Tomb of the Patriarchs ★★

The best-known monument in Hebron is the Tomb of the Patriarchs where **Abraham**, **Isaac** and **Jacob** are said to be buried. As a result, to Orthodox Jews, Hebron is the second most holy place after the Western Wall in Jerusalem. The Hebron area became the location of the Zionist settlement of **Kiryat Arba**, situated next to the Arab section of al-Khalil, which has frequently led to much fighting and harassment.

According to the Bible, Abraham paid for the site of the tomb, the **Cave of Machpelah**, as a burial chamber for his wife Sarah after he learnt that Adam and Eve were buried there. The structure covering the site, built in typical lavish style by Herod, dominates the centre of the town, and is a peculiar hybrid of various religions and architectural styles. Arabs put minarets onto the corners and the Crusaders turned the structure into a church, adding crenellations along the top. In 1188, the tomb became a mosque once more.

The interior is decorated with exquisite inlaid wood, intricate tiles and inscriptions from the Koran. A synagogue encased within the mosque exists for the benefit of Jewish worshippers. You can see all six tombs: Abraham and Sarah, Isaac and Rebecca, and Jacob and Leah. There is a **shrine to Joseph** at the entrance but Joseph's real remains are believed to be in Nablus, as stated in the Bible. Open 07:30–11:30; 13:30–17:00 daily except on Friday and Muslim holidays. Because of frequent trouble in Hebron, check with the tourist board in Jerusalem whether it is safe to visit before setting off.

JERICHO

The city of Jericho is located at 250m (820ft) below sea level. From Jerusalem, which sits high on an inland plain, the 30-minute drive takes place in steadily rising temperatures as the road descends through spectacular desert scenery of sand-coloured mountains, sculpted into weird shapes by years of water erosion.

Jericho itself lies on a lush, green oasis. An underground spring, **Ein al-Sultan** (The Spring of Elisha), is probably what drew the first settlers 10,000 years ago. The modern city, which sprawls lazily across the oasis, is very Arabic, many residents whiling away their time sipping strong coffee around the main square, gossiping or playing backgammon. The fruit markets are magnificent – everything here is bigger, brighter and juicier – and roadside stalls sell freshly squeezed, exotic juices like apricot or date, wonderfully refreshing in the heat. Food, too, is an adventure, with plenty of excellent, if basic, Middle Eastern restaurants to choose from.

The first settlement in Jericho is dated around 8000BC, some 4000 years before the Pyramids were built. It formed the first known example of man making the transition from hunter-gatherer to settler and farmer. From the mounds of soft earth at **Tel es-Sultan**, the excavations of the 23 ancient settlements, it's difficult to discern exactly what

> **THE INN OF THE GOOD SAMARITAN**
>
> The Parable of the Good Samaritan in *Luke* tells of the wounded Jew who was ignored by other travellers, most of them Samaritans, once sworn enemies of the Jews. However, one Samaritan stopped to help the traveller and took him to an inn. Although the story is fiction, a sign marks the spot, some 10km (6 miles) from the Mount of Olives on the Jericho Road, where the inn was supposed to have been. As traveller's inns were commonplace in the first century, the likelihood of some kind of building having existed here is strong.

Below: *Jericho's main square is deserted in the noon heat.*

was here, but the remains of a stone tower, some 7000 years old, indicate some sort of fortification. This is the spot where, according to the Bible, Joshua and the 'children of Israel' destroyed the then Canaanite city, around 1200BC, and the walls came tumbling down.

Hisham's Palace ★★

A few miles northeast of Jericho is the once-spectacular winter hunting lodge built by the **Ummayad Caliph** in AD724, during the Byzantine period. Little of the structure itself remains but there are some exquisite mosaics on the floor of the bathhouse, an indication of how lavish the structure must have been. A small museum houses fragments of pottery found on the site. Open 08:00–17:00, Monday–Thursday, Saturday; 08:00–16:00 Friday.

The Mount and Monastery of Temptation ★

Enthusiastic hikers should make the short journey out of town to the Greek Orthodox monastery on the Mount of Temptation, built to mark the spot where Jesus fasted in the desert for 40 days and 40 nights and where he was tempted by the Devil. The monastery is a short but steep uphill climb from the road, northwest of Jericho; it has a large collection of icons inside.

Below: *The Monastery of Temptation marks where Jesus fasted.*

Wadi Qelt ★★

This **wadi**, or dried-up riverbed, stretches for some 35km (20 miles) from Jerusalem to Jericho and is a **hiker's paradise** in winter. The landscape is spectacular: the warm ochre of the desert changes colour constantly as the sun moves across the sky, while the steep cliffs of the gorge, honeycombed with caves once inhabited by monks, are occasionally broken by a splash of bottle green where an underground spring emerges.

At the Jericho end of the wadi, the **Greek Orthodox Monastery of St George** clings to the side of the cliff with magnificent views over the plain and oasis below. The small community of monks will show visitors around from Monday to Saturday.

NORTH FROM JERUSALEM

Heading due north from Jerusalem via **Ramallah** and **Shofat**, a large Palestinian refugee camp, there's a trail of biblical sites. Be careful in this area; anti-Israeli sentiment runs high and there are outbreaks of trouble, so check the situation before joining a tour.

Above: *The Monastery of St George occupies a spectacular setting in Wadi Qelt.*

Beitin *

This neat little Arabic village is the biblical Beit El, where **Jacob** dreamed of a ladder ascending to Heaven and marked the spot with a pillar. There is not much to see, although some excavations have revealed what may have been Jacob's Temple.

Shiloh *

At Shiloh, a few kilometres further north, Israel was divided up between the 12 tribes and it is here that the **Ark of the Covenant** was kept for 200 years. There is not that much to view here either, but a small excavation has revealed **Bronze Age settlements** from 1600BC.

However, the scenery is beautiful as the road twists through mountains terraced with silvery olive groves, myrrh and tobacco. The **Valley of Dotan** on the way to Nablus is where Joseph's brothers sold him to the Egyptians as a slave.

Nablus *

Nablus is the largest city on the West Bank, with a population of approximately 100,000 inhabitants.

ISLAM

The Islamic religion stems from AD622 when the prophet Mohammed fled from Mecca to Medina. He went on to become an important religious and political leader. His scribbled writings, collected on fragments of fabric and bone, became the Koran, which presents the word of God, or Allah, in 114 chapters. The essential duties of a Muslim are: to have faith in Allah and his prophet, to pray facing Mecca, to fast during Ramadan, to give alms, and to make a pilgrimage to Mecca during his or her lifetime.

Known also as **Schechem**, Nablus is the site where **Jacob** pitched his tent and drank from a well. Muslims believe the real remains of Joseph are buried here, and not in Hebron, as has been commonly assumed.

Mount Gerezim ★

The lush, green hill to the southeast of Nablus is Mount Gerezim, which forms the heart of the Samaritan religion. Samaritans believe that Mount Gerezim was visible above the waters during the time of Noah and the Flood and that it was here, not in Jerusalem, that **Abraham** nearly sacrificed his son Isaac. Some 250 Samaritans spend the week of **Pesach** (Passover) on the mountain during which time lambs are sacrificed and cooked in the biblical way. Visitors can join a tour to witness the ceremony, although they are not allowed to see the actual sacrifices take place.

Sebastya ★★★

A further 10km (6 miles) to the north is the former capital of the Kingdom of Israel, Sebastya, where **King Omri** built luxurious palaces and temples in 880BC. Herod the Great later added the lavish **Temple of Augustus**. In the **Mosque of Nabi Yaya**, outside the village, are tombs of the prophets **Elisha** and **Obadiah** as well as the tomb of **John the Baptist**.

Right: *A watermelon seller in Nablus takes a break; like other towns in the West Bank, Nablus has suffered violent unrest in recent times and is not necessarily safe to visit. Tourists should be sure to check the political situation before venturing this far.*

The West Bank at a Glance

Spring and **autumn** are best because of high midsummer temperatures. Jericho, Bethlehem and Hebron get very hot in summer. The north part of the West Bank is slightly cooler. Winter evenings around East Jerusalem and Bethlehem can be cold, so take warm clothing.

The West Bank, or Occupied Territories, is only appropriate for a **day trip** and is best accessed from Jerusalem, the Dead Sea or Tel Aviv. Check the safety situation with the tourist office before entering the area. Their information will be pro-Israeli, but it is good to know in order to avoid trouble spots. From Jordan, the Allenby Bridge is the only border crossing. A 40km (27-mile) road through Israel links Gaza and the West Bank. Car passengers may only spend 90 minutes in Israeli territory between two points. Gaza International Airport opened in 1998, served by Palestinian Airlines and a handful of other regional services. The surrounding airspace is controlled by Israel, so only a limited number of flights are allowed in and out, although the Palestinian Authority is campaigning to change this.

If driving cars with yellow Israeli plates do not go into the Palestinian towns as you will be an easy target. There are clearly marked bypasses around all the towns. Otherwise, roads are good and the towns are well signposted. Arab buses, *sherut* (shared taxis), taxis and guided tours are the best way to get around. Don't stay after dark or break the curfews if you're driving independently. Buses to Jericho, Hebron and Bethlehem run from the **Suleiman Street Bus Station** in East Jerusalem.

Staying on the West Bank is not advised; tourists are recommended only to take day trips from Jerusalem on organized tours.

Most restaurants are simple falafal and hummous establishments where you can get a nice range of salads and Middle Eastern specialities. In Jericho, there are several places with gardens along En Es-Sultan Street and numerous fruit stalls dotted around the city selling freshly squeezed juice.

BUDGET

Al Andalus, Bethlehem. Located on Manger Square; serves both Eastern and Western dishes.
Mundo, Milk Grotto Street. Fast food, falafal and ice cream.

Egged Tours is Israel's largest bus company and operates day trips to places such as Bethlehem, from Tel Aviv and Jerusalem. It also operates from the bus stations of Eilat, Tiberias and Haifa.
Egged Tours, Jaffa Road, Jerusalem, tel: (02) 525-3454.

Tourist Information, 17 Jaffa Road, tel: (02) 625-8844.
British Consulate General, Jerusalem, tel: (02) 582-8281; East Jerusalem, tel: (02) 582-8263.
US Consulate General, Jerusalem, tel: (02) 625-3288.

4
Tel Aviv

Israel's city on the beach is home to some two million people, or 40% of the country's population. Less than 100 years old, Tel Aviv's eclectic architectural style reflects the many new waves of immigrants: their dreams of recreating the neoclassical grace of Vienna, ornate experimentation with Art Nouveau and the minimalist lines of Bauhaus style. In amongst this unlikely collection of buildings, the traffic roars, the cafés buzz with conversation and the working population goes about its frenetic daily business. After work and at weekends everybody heads for the city's beaches, to swim, sunbathe or simply stroll along the promenade.

Any visitor thirsting for a bit of history can venture slightly south to **Jaffa**, one of the world's oldest cities steeped in biblical tales and mythology. A colourful artistic community thrives here today. In addition, Jaffa offers a fine line in nightlife, with lively bars and clubs open well into the small hours.

To the north of the Tel Aviv–Jaffa area, along the sweeping expanse of the Mediterranean beaches, is Israel's exclusive resort of **Herzliya**, haunt of the rich and beautiful, as well as **Netanya**, heart of the country's important diamond-cutting industry. Southwest is **Rishon le-Zion**, set amongst rolling vineyards, and **Ashkelon**, birthplace of Herod the Great.

Tel Aviv also makes a convenient base for exploring the rest of the country; Israel's main international airport, Ben-Gurion, is located nearby, while Jerusalem, for example, is only 30 minutes along the motorway.

DON'T MISS

★★★ **Jaffa:** visit the world's oldest working harbour which has great views of the bay.
★★★ **Beth Hatefutsoth Museum:** tells the story of the Diaspora.
★★ **Carmel Market:** experience the hustle and bustle of the market.
★★ **National Antiquities Park:** explore magnificent ruins at Ashkelon.
★★ **Rishon le-Zion:** taste wonderful wines.
★ **Netanya:** window-shop for diamonds.

Opposite: *Extensive sandy beaches line modern Tel Aviv.*

THE SLAYING OF RABIN

Prime Minister Yitzhak Rabin, head of the Labour Party, was assassinated in 1995 in the now-renamed Yitzhak Rabin Square. Speaking at a peace rally, he was shot by an ultra-right-wing Jewish student. Instrumental in the 1990s peace process, Rabin was highly respected worldwide. The square has been covered in graffiti since his death.

TEL AVIV

Tel Aviv is actually the first Jewish city to have been built in 2000 years. In 1909, a group of families from the rather overcrowded, predominantly Arab port of Jaffa staked their claim on the sand dunes to the north. The new suburb which they created – named Tel Aviv, or Hill of Hope – expanded rapidly until, in 1948, it became the capital of Israel. Today, big hotels tower over Tel Aviv's beaches, while Dizengoff Street and Dizengoff Square, named after the city's founder and first mayor Meir Dizengoff, are centres for *haute couture* shopping, eating and nightlife.

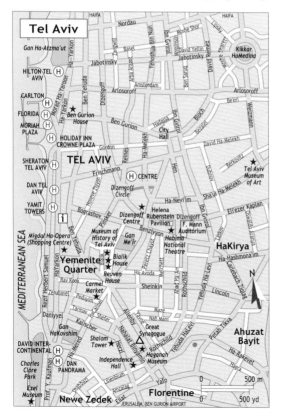

The Shalom Tower ★★

Soaring 35 stories above **Herzl Street**, this tower is one of Israel's tallest buildings, a good place to orientate yourself and to see just how small the country is. From the observatory on the top (30th floor) you can see on a clear day the Negev Desert to the south, Jerusalem to the east and the Carmel Mountains to the north. On the third floor there's a small **Wax Museum** of effigies of key Israeli figures over the last century. Open 10:00–18:30 Sunday–Thursday, 10:00–14:00 Friday, 11:00–16:00 Saturday. The Shalom Tower stands on the former site of the **Herzliya Gymnasium**, the first school of the new town, erected in 1909.

Yemenite Quarter *

In the shadow of the Shalom Tower lies the bustling Yemenite Quarter, which hasn't changed much over the last 100 years. Low-rise stone houses line the noisy, narrow streets, all with a distinctly Arabic flavour. Some of the best Middle Eastern restaurants in the city are located here, specializing in pungent Yemenite cuisine.

Carmel Market **

Close by, around HaCarmel Street, is the colourful Carmel Street Market, a riot of sights, sounds and smells. Fragrant herbs, juicy piles of fruits, sumptuous green vegetables and more exotic specimens like yellow star fruit and piles of glistening dates are all on sale alongside clothes and kitchenware, and the aromas of freshly baked pitta and the ubiquitous fried falafal wafting by.

Rothschild Boulevard **

Tel Aviv has a rich and lively cultural life, the hub of which is Rothschild Boulevard. As well as being a desirable address, this broad, tree-lined street, one of the first in the city, embraces several architectural styles. Number 16 is **Independence Hall**, former residence of Meir Dizengoff, in which the independent State of Israel was declared by the then prime minister, David Ben-Gurion. Open 09:00–14:00 Sunday–Thursday. The

Above: *Carmel Market is a medley of colours, sights and smells.*
Below left: *Tel Aviv seen from the Shalom Tower.*

MINISTER MEIR

Golda Meir (1898–1978) was one of the founders of the State of Israel. While in her teens she became a Zionist and in 1921 she and her husband immigrated to Palestine. She was a signatory to the Proclamation of the Independence of the State of Israel in 1948 and served as her country's first minister to the USSR, as well as minister of labour and social insurance for Israel. In 1956 she became minister of foreign affairs. She served, successively, as secretary-general of the Mapai Party and of the United Israel Labour Party from 1966–68. She was prime minister from 1969 to 1974, when she resigned amid controversy over Israel's lack of preparedness in the Yom Kippur War of 1973.

Above: *Dizengoff Circle, a focal point of Tel Aviv.*

peculiar mix of styles of **No. 46** – ornate balconies and a minaret – attracted the attention of the Soviet Ambassador, who chose to base the embassy there until diplomatic relations were severed in 1953.

The Haganah Museum at No. 23 provides a fascinating glimpse into the methods used by the Israeli Defence Force in manufacturing arms and concealing them from the British when Palestine was under British Mandate. Numbers 89 and 91, meanwhile, are typical examples of the German **Bauhaus** school of architecture. Open 09:00–16:00 Sunday–Thursday.

At the northern end of the street, the **Mann Auditorium** is the home of the **Israeli Philharmonic Orchestra** and the **Habima Theatre**, one of the first theatres to stage performances in Hebrew.

Dizengoff Street ★★★

The fashion and food highlight of Tel Aviv, this glamorous boulevard is the place to sit in a pavement café and people-watch or to browse through the many chic designer shops. Eat your way through delicious Viennese pastries, fruit-juice cocktails, Hungarian blinis, pastrami and falafal and watch a never-ending fashion parade, at its most exotic on Friday evenings, as Tel Aviv gathers and decides where to party that night.

The focal point of all this is **Dizengoff Circle**, a raised piazza with an unusual fountain at its centre. The fountain is a series of coloured, cog-like rings which rotate. Every hour, on the hour, there's a musical display with jets of water and a flame. A few streets to the south is the **Dizengoff Centre**, a busy shopping centre complete with restaurants and cinemas.

PEACE AND QUIET IN TEL AVIV

Tel Aviv and Jaffa have a number of pretty parks and gardens for visitors to explore or in which to have a few moments' rest.
• **Gan Meir:** small, attractive park off Bialik Street.
• **Clore Park:** green patch between the beach and the Dan Panorama hotel. Clean sand and usually not too many people.
• **Ha-Yarkon Park:** big recreational area along the Yarkon River, north of the city centre. Boating pond, grassy areas and, in summer, free outdoor concerts.
• **Independence Park:** behind the Sheraton and the Hilton. Gay hangout in the evenings.

Tel Aviv Museum of Art ★★

Also in this area are the three buildings of the **Tel Aviv Museum of Art**. The **Helena Rubenstein Pavilion** at the top of Rothschild Boulevard houses temporary exhibitions of contemporary art. Nearby there's the **Art Education Centre** and on Sha'ul Ha-Melekh Boulevard is the museum's main building, with permanent collections of Israeli and modern art and a large European section from the 16th to the 19th centuries. Prize exhibits include work by Picasso, Renoir, Munch and Roy Lichtenstein. Open 10:00–16:00 Monday, Wednesday, Saturday; 10:00–22:00 Tuesday, Thursday; 10:00–14:00 Friday; closed Sunday.

Beth Hatefutsoth Museum ★★★

Anybody wishing to understand the **Diaspora**, the worldwide dispersion of the Jewish people, should visit the fascinating Beth Hatefutsoth Museum on the Tel Aviv University Campus. Scale models and interactive displays tell the story from the beginning of the Diaspora to the return to Zion, showing what life was like for Jews in overseas non-Jewish communities and the impression the Jews made on these places. The audiovisual show of Jewish migration around the world slots the Diaspora into world history and visitors can select from documentaries listed in a catalogue. There's even a computer system through which those with Jewish ancestry can trace their lineage. Open 10:00–16:00, Monday, Tuesday, Thursday; 10:00–18:00 Wednesday; closed on Friday and Saturday.

Beaches ★

Tel Aviv is unusual in that there are great beaches – for most of the time safe to swim from and pleasantly uncrowded – right on its doorstep. Broad, sandy and very clean, the beaches in front of the **Hilton** all the way south to the **Charles Clore Park** are patrolled by lifeguards. Windsurfing, sailing and jet skis are available for hire.

> ### GOLDEN SANDS
>
> Tel Aviv's coast can have strong **undercurrents**, so never swim when the black flag is flying and be careful if the red one is raised. Be careful of valuables; while violent crime is uncommon in Israel, there's plenty of petty theft. Many of the beaches have deck chairs and lockers to rent. Beware, however, of flying objects. Paddleball, or *matzkot*, is a national passion. Players have round wooden bats and hit the ball back and forth, making frequent enthusiastic dives into the sand.

Below: *Striking Dizengoff Centre is packed with shops and restaurants.*

SCENTS OF CITRUS

Citrus fruit is Israel's most valuable agricultural export, yet is not indigenous to the country. The coastal strip, which now presents ideal growing conditions, was until 150 years ago a malaria-infested swamp. It was the hardy pioneers in the last century who installed pumps to drain the swamps and pump up fresh water for the fledgling orchards. Jaffa eventually became the most important port for citrus, hence the name **Jaffa Oranges**, and today, acres of scented orange, lemon and grapefruit groves line the coast.

JAFFA

Jaffa is everything the visitor could hope for in a picturesque Mediterranean port: a cluster of old houses clinging to the hillside above the harbour; colourful fishing boats unloading their daily catch; an offbeat artistic community; and, of course, spectacular fish restaurants.

Unlike modern Tel Aviv, Jaffa's history stretches back thousands of years. Jaffa is Hebrew for 'beautiful', and was given to the port by Noah's youngest son, Japheth, who decided to settle here after the great Flood had subsided. The prophet **Jonah** fled to Tarshish from Jaffa, encountering a whale along the way, and cedars of Lebanon were once offloaded at this ancient harbour for the construction of Solomon's Temple in Jerusalem.

Jaffa thrived as a port for an astonishing 4000 years, being invaded, knocked down and rebuilt at least 15 times. Under British Mandate, however, Haifa became Israel's main port and Jaffa fell into decline. Realizing its potential as a tourist attraction in 1963, the city of Tel Aviv reconstructed the old streets using local, honey-coloured stone and a distinctly Middle Eastern style.

There are plenty of street vendors and a disproportionate amount of bakeries, and the air is permanently filled with mouthwatering wafts of freshly baked bread, which often comes in different flavours. Jaffa is quite touristy, with a fair number of bars cashing in on the legend of Perseus and Andromeda, for which this was supposedly the setting (*see* panel opposite).

Exploring Jaffa on foot ★★★

Jaffa is quite a sprawling place, but the old, walled area, which contains all the interesting sites, is easy to cover on foot. Start at the **Ottoman Clocktower**, dating back to 1906, on Yefet Street. A series of stained glass windows around the tower tells the story of the town's history. The courtyard opposite was once an Armenian hostel, a kind of staging post for travellers going to and from the Jewish settlements inland. Further along the road, past the police station, is the **Al-Mahamoudia Mosque**, built in 1812 and named after the Turkish governor. Non-Muslims are not allowed inside.

A block to the right, heading towards the sea, is Jaffa's **Museum of Antiquities**. The fruits of 20 years of excavations are displayed here, giving a good insight into Jaffa's colourful past. The 18th-century building has had many uses; first it was the Turkish governor's headquarters, then a prison and later, a soap factory. Open 09:00–13:00 Sunday–Thursday.

Next door, the **Saint Louis Monastery** in the court-yard of **St Peter's Church** is named after King Louis IX

Above: *Old Jaffa, a must for any visitor to Tel Aviv.*

ANDROMEDA'S ROCK

The Greek myth of Perseus and Andromeda comes from the old port of Jaffa. Legend has it that the king of Jaffa (in some indeterminate period of history) chained his beautiful daughter Andromeda to a rock outside the port to appease a particularly vicious sea monster. Perseus, on his winged white horse, snatched Andromeda from the jaws of death and bore her off into the sunset. Some 2000 years ago, residents of the port even believed that the chains that bound Andromeda and the skeleton of the monster were visible in the sea.

SUNSET STROLLS

Why not take a sunset stroll along the beach to Jaffa? The old port is visible all the way along the wide, sandy strip and the walk is marvellously invigorating after a day's sightseeing in the heat. Once you arrive at Jaffa, simply climb over the hill to the main square, lined with bars and restaurants.

Below: *Jaffa's clock tower is an ideal meeting place.*

of France who stayed here in 1147 during the Seventh Crusade. Later, the monastery became a hostel for pilgrims and even accommodated Napoleon who decided to relax here for a while after conquering Jaffa.

Further towards the sea, next to the minaret of the **Jama El-Baher Mosque**, is the first Jewish house in Jaffa built in 1820, which doubled up as a hostel for visitors from Jerusalem. There was an Armenian inn here, too, now marked by a convent.

Past the **HaPisgah gardens**, a grassy area where you can rest in the shade, the **Horoscope Path** begins, following the contours of the Old City wall to the red-and-white-striped **lighthouse**. From the path you can see into houses, galleries and artists' studios. Next to the lighthouse is the biblical **house** of **Simon the Tanner**, where the apostle Peter performed a healing miracle. Open 08:00–11:45, then 14:00–16:00 (14:00–18:30 in summer) daily. **Kedumin Square** in the renovated part of town is worth a visit: you can actually see the layers of Jaffa in the excavations.

Jaffa's other main attraction is the famous flea market, **Shuk HaPishpishim**, where all manner of junk and dubious 'authentic' crafts are sold: Persian rugs, leather bags and jackets, paintings, pots and pieces in brass. An antique here is probably not a genuine antique and it's important to remember that haggling is the only way to arrive at a remotely realistic price.

After touring Jaffa, which is particularly beautiful as the setting sun turns the old buildings into a shade of amber – consider staying for dinner in one of the excellent fish restaurants. Alternatively, in summer, try walking along the beach and enjoy the sunset from the sands.

NIGHTLIFE

As well as **Jaffa**, with its seafood restaurants, bars and clubs, many of which stay open into the small hours, Tel Aviv has two other focal points for nightlife. After a drink on Dizengoff Street, people move to **North Tel Aviv**, a relatively new, fashionable centre of clubs, bars and restaurants roughly where Dizengoff, Ben Yehuda and Ha-Yarkhon streets converge. Anything from Asian to European food is available and there's a great atmosphere for strolling around.

The most fashionable of all Tel Aviv's night-time hubs is the **Promenade**, a wide pedestrian zone that borders the city's beautiful beaches. As late as October, the outdoor restaurants and bars here are packed with people late into the night and the walkway is alive with magicians, buskers and artists.

Above: *The narrow old streets of Jaffa are an artist's dream.*

Below left: *Jaffa harbour contains several superb fish restaurants.*

WOMEN TRAVELLERS

Israel is a remarkably trouble-free place in which to travel alone. In Tel Aviv, it is quite acceptable to go out for dinner alone or visit the theatre or cinema. The beach is safe until late at night and is busy in the warmer months until after midnight with men and women jogging, sitting on the sand or walking their dogs. If strangers do try to chat to you, they're usually harmless; violent crime and drug problems are very rare. Do be careful when hitch-hiking alone, though.

Below: *The magnificent beaches of Tel Aviv are a joy for the family.*

DAY TRIPS FROM TEL AVIV

Long, sandy beaches stretch in an unbroken line south from Tel Aviv to the Gaza Strip. The beaches near the towns can sometimes be busy, as Israelis take refuge from the summer humidity to indulge in sunbathing, windsurfing or swimming.

Rishon le-Zion **

A short drive southeast from Tel Aviv, Rishon le-Zion was one of the first new Jewish settlements in Israel. The name, which means 'First in Zion', was coined by a group of Russian and Polish Jews who arrived here in 1882, fleeing the pogroms of Eastern Europe.

Life in the new country was not much easier, as the settlers were inexperienced farmers and had to contend with malarial swamps, pirate raids and disease. After five years, the French philanthropist, Baron Edmond de Rothschild, came to the settlers' aid by sending a team of experts to start a vineyard and providing the necessary financial assistance. They arrived armed with shoots of Bordeaux, Beaujolais and Burgundy grapevines and Israel's wine industry was born.

The first wines were mainly sweet, made for Jewish religious holidays, but by 1957, when Rothschild relinquished control and the **Carmel Oriental Vineyard Company** was started, a range of delicious dry whites and table wines was being produced as well. Visitors can tour the cellars and enjoy a free tasting. The vineyard's pretty garden contains seven trees from biblical times: fig, date, grape, pomegranate, olive, palm and carob. The cellars are open 10:00–17:00 Monday–Thursday, Saturday–Sunday.

On the way back to Tel Aviv, visit the beach resort of **Bat Yam** for a swim. The beaches here are broad, clean and surprisingly uncrowded.

Ashkelon ★★

Israel's most southerly resort town, Ashkelon stretches out along 12km (7½ miles) of beautiful sandy beach. The town is pleasant if modern. Ashkelon's origins, however, date back 4000 years to when it was an important Philistine city-state. As a trading port on the Via Maris, the coast road linking Egypt and Syria, Ashkelon exported wine and grain and consequently became much desired by Assyrians,

Above: *Women as well as men must serve in Israel's Defence Force.*

Babylonians, Greeks, Romans, Arabs and Crusaders. Buildings, statues and columns have been uncovered by archaeologists and there are some awe-inspiring sights casually scattered around (such as the toppled Roman pillars lying in frothy surf at the base of the sand dunes), but as yet the ancient ruins of Ashkelon's original city-state have not been discovered.

National Antiquities Park ★★

Part theme park, part excavations, this shoreside park is littered with ancient pillars, columns and statues. A grassy wall, built by the Crusaders, surrounds the site, while the beach forms the other border. Visitors can wander freely through the ruins and reconstructed **Roman columns** and roads, and look at the **Sculpture Corner** in the park, where some of the archaeologists' finds are displayed.

Painted Tomb ★

Near the town centre, on the beach, is a Roman tomb some 1700 years old, depicting scenes from the after-life and worth a quick look. Open 09:00–15:00 daily.

ASHKELON FACTS

• Ashkelon is where star-crossed lovers **Samson** and **Delilah** had their ill-fated romance: he was a Jew and she was the Philistine who betrayed him. Each has a beach named after them today.
• **King Herod the Great** was supposedly born in Ashkelon.
• A special kind of onion has been grown here for 3000 years and named **scallion** after the town.
• The part of the town named **Afridar** was founded by a group of South African Jews escaping the apartheid regime in the 1950s.

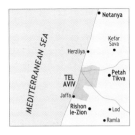

Herzliya **

North of Tel Aviv, the ritzy resort of Herzliya which was named after Theodor Herzl, the founder of Zionism, is the playground of Israel's wealthy. A popular weekend retreat from Tel Aviv for those lucky enough to afford a villa here, Herzliya is packed with gourmet restaurants, deluxe hotels and fashionable cafés, strung out along beautiful beaches crammed with tanning bodies in summer. Some of the beaches charge an entrance fee and some have special functions: **Shefayim** is a nudist beach while, at the other end of the scale, **Separate Beach** is the religious beach. Outside the city, a zone of high-tech companies has sprung up, many of them in the communications business. Plush villas, inhabited by entrepreneurs, line the low hills overlooking the Mediterranean.

People, not ruins, are what visitors come to Herzliya to see, but there is one rather crumbling historical site nearby at **Arshaf**. The Greeks built a port here called **Appollonia**, of which nothing but a part of a jetty remains. There's a 12th-century Crusader fort nearby, though no signs remain of the battle fought here between Richard the Lionheart and Saladin during the Crusader era. The fort was destroyed later by the Mamelukes. Some people claim the sandy beach contains fragments of purple-coloured glass, dating back to the seventh century AD when a huge factory was built at Hadera, some distance to the north.

Netanya ★★

Some distance further to the north, Netanya is a bustling and less ostentatious beach resort nestling behind a long line of scrub-covered sand dunes. Netanya is the centre for Israel's two biggest foreign exchange earners, citrus and diamond polishing. The town was founded in 1929 amidst the citrus groves, and the diamond

business was brought to Netanya by immigrant Belgian and Dutch Jews, already skilled in polishing and cutting.

In winter, the resort is dead but summer sees a lively cultural programme of international movies, folklore shows and singing in the modern amphitheatre in **Gan Ha-Melekh Park**, right on the beach. As well as watersports, there's horse-riding outside the town. For something different, visitors can see a **citrus-packing plant** in action or have supper with an Israeli family, which can be arranged through the tourist office.

Netanya Diamond Centre ★★

Whether or not you are in the market for a diamond, the Netanya Diamond Centre on Herzl Boulevard is a fascinating insight into the glamorous world of diamonds. The visit is fun for children too – there's a scale model of a South African diamond mine with a model railway, and a museum of exhibits from raw lumps of rock to glittering stones. The large collection of finished products is tempting but expensive.

Above: *Succulent olives on sale in Netanya; the town is also well known for citrus fruits.*
Opposite: *Don't expect to find much empty sand on beaches outside Tel Aviv on a Saturday.*
Below: *An eye for detail is needed to cut the precious stones at the Netanya Diamond Centre.*

Tel Aviv at a Glance

Tel Aviv enjoys a **balmy** climate all year round, although summer is best avoided as it can get very **humid** and oppressive. From **April** to **October**, the weather is warm enough to enjoy the beaches and swimming in the Mediterranean. September is the main period of Jewish holidays, during which time many attractions will be closed for the occasional day.

Tel Aviv is the location of Israel's main **airport**, Ben-Gurion, situated 20km (12½ miles) southeast of the city. **Buses** run from the airport terminal to the city centre, passing the main hotel area on the beach, the youth hostel and the railway station. For timetable information, tel: (03) 971-1886.
The domestic airline, **Arkia**, operates flights to Jerusalem, Eilat and Rosh Pinna from **Sde Dov**, the domestic airport, tel: (03) 698-4500. El-Rom Airline also runs an air taxi service, tel: (03) 541-2554.

Buses run all over the city, operated by **Egged**, tel: (03) 527-1212, and **Dan**, tel: (03) 639-4444. There are Egged services to Ashdod and Ashkelon in the south. Alternatively, travel by *sherut* or **taxi**, or walk along the beach

to Jaffa. Tel Aviv has **two railway stations**: the Central Railway Station serves Haifa via Netanya and another station south of the Central Bus Station serves Jerusalem on Kibbutz Galuyot Road.

All the big hotels are along Ha-Yarkon on the beach, for which there is naturally a premium to pay. Tel Aviv also has a good selection of budget accommodation and a youth hostel.

LUXURY

Tel Aviv Hilton, Independence Park, Tel Aviv 63405, tel: (03) 520-2240, concierge.telaviv@hilton.com Big, modern hotel on the beach surrounded on three sides by a park. All facilities and extensive business amenities.

David Inter-Continental, 12 Kaufman Street, Tel Aviv 61501, tel: (03) 795-1111, telaviv@interconti.com Luxury five-star hotel on the seafront, ideal for all travellers.

Dan Tel Aviv Hotel, 99 Ha-Yarkon Street, Tel Aviv 63903, tel: (03) 520-2525, dantelaviv@danhotels.com One of the city's most prestigious hotels, with every conceivable luxury, located on the seafront.

MID-RANGE

Hotel Imperial, 66 Ha-Yarkon Street, Tel Aviv 63902, tel: (03) 517-7002, imperial1@012.net.il Com-

fortable two-star hotel on the beach. Good coffee shop.

City Hotel, 9 Mapu Street, Tel Aviv 63566, tel: (03) 524-6253, reservations@atlashotels.co.il Three-star hotel, in the city centre, can walk to the beach.

Armon Hayarkon, 268 Ha-Yarkon Street, tel: (03) 605-5271, info@armon-hotel.co.il Small, modern hotel on main beachfront road.

BUDGET

Petach Tikva, Tahalom Street, Petach Tikva, tel: (03) 922-6660, petachtikva@iyha.org.il Small youth hostel in quiet suburb, near airport.

Bnei Dan Guesthouse, 36 Bnei Dan Street, tel: (03) 544-1748, telaviv@iyha.org.il Clean, comfortable youth hostel (with café).

Tel Aviv has lots of restaurants, many of them excellent. The most elegant – and expensive – dining tends to be in the big hotels. North Tel Aviv and Dizengoff Street are both filled with places to eat and drink, for the best fish, head for Jaffa. Travellers on a budget should eat at the Central Bus Station if passing through; the street vendors there serve amazingly cheap falafal and chips. More pleasant are the many bars and restaurants springing up along the Promenade.

LUXURY

Baobab, 43 Ahad Ha-Am Street, Tel Aviv, tel: (03) 566-3331.

International and Israeli cuisine. Very fashionable.
Casaba, 32 Yirmiyahu Street, tel: (03) 604-2617. Upmarket international cuisine.

MID-RANGE
Manta Ray, Tel Aviv Promenade, tel: (03) 517-4773. Seafood and mezze on the beach.

BUDGET
Hakkosem, 1 Shlomo Hamelech, tel: (03) 525-2033. Fantastic falafal!
Zion, 28 Peduim Street, tel: (03) 517-8714. Basic but interesting Yemenite food in the Yemenite Quarter.

SHOPPING

Tel Aviv has four fine shopping malls: the **Dizengoff Centre**, **Gan Ha'Ir** (next to the City Hall), a mall at the bus terminal on Levinski Street, and one at the **Opera Tower** on Allenby Street. The city's markets are also worth a browse. On Tuesdays and Fridays there's an arts and crafts bazaar at Nahalat Binyamin Pedestrian Mall. Open 10:00–16:00 daily. Also don't miss the **Carmel Market** in Tel Aviv and **Shuk HaPishpishim**, the flea market in Jaffa.

TOURS AND EXCURSIONS

All the main tour operators run excursions from Tel Aviv all over Israel, by air-conditioned coach, minibus or jeep. **Day trips** operate to Caesarea, Akko and Galilee; the Dead Sea and Masada;

and, of course, Jerusalem and Bethlehem, just an hour away by road. **Egged** runs guided tours in several languages as part of its 'eye opener' programme, tel: (03) 527-1212. The company also operates a daily bus to Cairo. **Tracks** runs adventure tours and overland treks all over Israel, tel: (03) 691-6103. There are various free entertainments in Tel Aviv. For a full list of what's on, see the Friday edition of the *Jerusalem Post*. At 09:30 on Wednesdays there's a free walking tour of Jaffa in English, starting from the clock tower, tel: (03) 682-6796. From 11:00–15:00 on Saturdays, enjoy Israeli folk dancing on the Promenade at **Ben & Jerry's**, near the Ramada Hotel. Entrance to the beaches is free apart from Tel Baruch and Hof Hatzuk. Beaches are supervized from April until mid-October. For times, tel: (03) 604-4955. Self-guided walking tours start from 5 Shalom Aleichem Street, from where orange posts mark out four different routes. Big pop and rock concerts take place in Ha-

Yarkon park, many featuring internationally famous bands. Concerts often take place in the open air and the atmosphere on a warm night is wonderful.

USEFUL CONTACTS

Tourist information:
Tel Aviv: 5 Ben Gurion, tel: (03) 639-5660.
Netanya: Haatzma'ut Square, tel: (09) 882-7286.
Cameri Theatre,
tel: (03) 523-3335;
There are Hebrew plays every Tuesday with simultaneous translation into English.
Habima Theatre,
tel: (03) 629-5555; Israel's national theatre.
Mann Auditorium,
tel: (03) 525-1502;
home of the Israel Philharmonic.
Tel Aviv Centre of the Performing Arts,
tel: (03) 692-7777;
home of the New Israeli Opera.
You will find that all the main **car rental** companies have offices in Tel Aviv:
Avis, tel: (03) 527-1752;
Hertz, tel: (03) 684-1011;
Thrifty, tel: (03) 561-2050.

TEL AVIV	J	F	M	A	M	J	J	A	S	O	N	D
AVERAGE TEMP. °F	65	66	68	72	77	83	86	86	89	84	76	66
AVERAGE TEMP. °C	18	19	20	22	25	28	30	30	31	29	24	19
Hours of sun daily	7	7	8	10	11	14	13	13	12	8	7	6
RAINFALL in	3.1	3.1	2.2	.6	0	0	0	0	0	.63	1.9	2.3
RAINFALL mm	80	80	56	15	0	0	0	0	0	16	48	62
Days of rainfall	11	11	8	4	0	0	0	0	0	5	10	11

5
The Dead Sea and Negev

Yet another of Israel's many unusual experiences, the Dead Sea is a must for every visitor. While the water is 'dead' – it harbours no life – the region is stunningly beautiful: the yellow mountains of the **Judean Desert** roll into a hazy blue sky, with the occasional splash of brilliant green heralding a kibbutz. Along the shoreline are two deeply important sites: **Qumran**, where the **Dead Sea Scrolls**, the oldest documents known to man, were discovered and tragic **Masada**, the one-time mountain fortress of the ill-fated **Zealots**.

The Judean Desert merges into the dusty **Negev**, which blends into the Egyptian Sinai. The Negev is gaining a reputation for adventure travel such as trekking, camel riding, abseiling and survival experiences. The surprisingly lush *wadis* (seasonal riverbeds) are home to all kinds of wildlife, and in places underground springs have been tapped to bring the desert into bloom. In the central Negev, a string of unusual craters, the best known of which is **Maktesh Ramon** (in the town of Mitzpe Ramon), attracts growing numbers of tourists.

In the far south, where Israel narrows down to the point of a V, is **Eilat**, about as far removed from the country's sombre religious and historical sites as it is possible to get, although sadly it has not proven immune from terrorist attacks. Big, brash and lively, it's packed with tourist hotels and nightlife. Should they so wish, visitors can now fly in and out of the so-called Red Sea Riviera and not go within miles of a temple or ruin for their entire stay.

DON'T MISS

*** Dead Sea: enjoy the Israel cliché: float on the sea.
*** Masada: evocative ruins.
** Eilat: swim with dolphins.
** Desert Safari: see the area by jeep or by camel.
** The Hai-Bar Nature Reserve: great wildlife tours.
** Qumran: the site where the Dead Sea Scrolls were discovered.
** Ein Gedi waterfalls: near the Dead Sea – not to be missed.

Opposite: *The desert becomes harsher and hotter as the road descends to the Dead Sea.*

THE SALTY SEA

The reason we can **float** on the Dead Sea is because of its concentration of solid substances. Six times as salty as the ocean, the Dead Sea contains 27% of solids of sodium chloride (common salt), magnesium chloride, calcium chloride, potassium chloride, bromine and more. The lake contains no life except for a few kinds of microbes; sea fish put into its waters soon die. The Dead Sea is economically import-ant as a source of potash, bromine, gypsum, salt, and other chemical products.

Below: *Follow the rules when swimming in the Dead Sea or you may just be in for an unwelcome surprise.*

THE DEAD SEA IS COMPLETELY
SAFE IF YOU FOLLOW SOME SIMPLE RULES

USE THE STEPS WHILE GETTING INTO THE WATER.

FIRST TAKE A SITTING POSITION, AND THEN
LIE ON YOUR BACK.

DON'T ATTEMPT ANY BREAST STROKE,
YOUR HEAD MIGHT SINK AND IT'S DANGEROUS.

IF SOME WATER GETS INTO YOUR EYES
DON'T PANIC LIE QUIETLY ON YOUR BACK
AND THE PAIN WILL PASS.

DON'T SPLASH, ESPECIALLY NOT ON OTHERS.

IT'S STRICTLY FORBIDDEN TO DRINK THE WATER.
IF BY MISTAKE YOU SWALLOW SOME WATER
GO AT ONCE TO THE OFFICE AND GET A DRINK.

USE ONLY THE MARKED ZONE.

CLOSED ON SABBATH & HOLYDAYS.

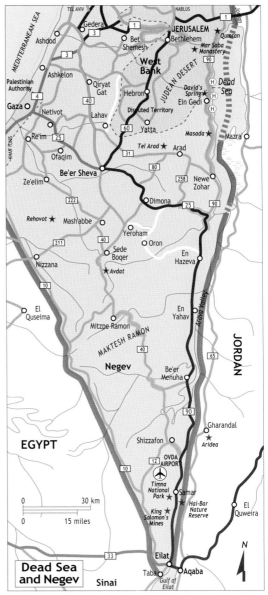

TEL AVIV   NABLUS

Gedera
Ashdod   Bet   JERUSALEM
          Shemesh   Bethlehem   Qumran
                              Mar Saba
MEDITERRANEAN SEA   West   Monastery
                    Bank   Dead
Ashkelon   JUDEAN DESERT   Sea
Palestinian   David's
Authority   Qiryat   Springs
          Gat   Hebron   Ein Gedi
Gaza   Netivot   Disputed Territory
          Lahav
Re'im   Yatta
          Ofaqim   Masada
                    Tel Arad   Mazra
          Be'er Sheva   Arad
Ze'elim   Newe
                    Zohar
          Dimona
          Rehovot   Mash'abbe
                    Yeroham
          Sede   Oron
          Boqer   En
Nizzana   Hazeva
          Avdat

El   En
Quseima   Yahav
          Mitzpe Ramon   JORDAN
          MAKTESH RAMON
          Negev   Be'er
                    Menuha

          Gharandal
EGYPT   Shizzafon   Aridea
          OVDA
          AIRPORT
          Timna
          National   Samar
          Park   Hai-Bar   El
0   30 km   King   Nature   Quweira
          Solomon's   Reserve
0   15 miles   Mines

Dead Sea   Eilat
and Negev   Taba   Aqaba
          Sinai   Gulf of
               Eilat

N

THE DEAD SEA

The lowest point on earth at about 400m (1300ft) below sea level, the Dead Sea is fascinating. In winter, the dry air, balmy climate and pure atmosphere make a visit an absolute joy. In summer, as you descend through the mountains from Jerusalem past the sign saying 'sea level', a wall of heat hits you in the face.

The Dead Sea is actually composed of two shimmering blue lakes, linked by a canal, and fed by the **River Jordan** from the north; it is surrounded by steep, barren mountains which turn into an incredible shade of mauve at sunset. Sparkling chunks of salt crystals float on the lake and the shoreline in places consists of glistening black mud, which health-mad tourists delight in slapping all over their bodies. A number of health spas have sprung up along the shores, although the occasional dilapidated ruin sitting in the middle of the bleached desert is testimony to the fact that the lake is shrinking fast, mainly as a result of the construction of Israel's National Carrier system and a similar Jordanian water system, a source of alarm to both Israel and Jordan (which lies along the eastern shore). Israel has created a series of artificial lakes at the southern end of the Dead Sea for the extraction of potash, but otherwise the land is used for campsites and health spas, promising to cure everything from arthritis to psoriasis.

The Dead Sea has always been a short-term visit for all but the most dedicated of spa-goers. Nevertheless, a host of new facilities and luxury hotels is gradually turning the area into a thriving holiday destination, with nightlife, restaurants and new beaches.

Below: *Visitors come to relax at the lowest point on earth.*

Qumran ★★

A network of dusty canyons 100m (300ft) above the Dead Sea, Qumran is where the **Dead Sea Scrolls** were found in 1947. The area was a settlement of the religious sect, the **Essenes**, who wrote the scrolls, and today Qumran has been designated as a national park. A few remains of the settlement can be seen: a tower and a few rooms as well as the pretty oasis of **Ein Feshkha** to the south, where the locals cultivated their vegetable crops. Try to visit at sunset to get a feel for the silence of the desert and the emptiness of the place.

The Essene people who made Qumran their headquarters in around 150BC were a very strict religious sect who lived a simple, monastic lifestyle in all-male communities. Women had to be 'pure' to produce an Essene child and apart from reproduction, had no place in the community. The Essenes predicted the end of the world to be a battle between the Sons of Darkness and the Sons of Light. This idea is illustrated at the Israel Museum in Jerusalem by a black marble slab placed alongside the white Shrine of the Book that today houses the Dead Sea Scrolls.

The scrolls revealed a great deal about Essene life and philosophy and threw new light on the **Second Temple Period**, as well as illustrating anti-Roman feeling among Jews at the time. However, in the first **Jewish War** in AD88, Essene history came to an abrupt end when the sect was tragically wiped out by the Romans. A sound and light show tells the whole story. Open 08:00–17:00 Monday–Thursday. Saturday–Sunday.

Ein Gedi ★★

Ein Gedi is a beautiful nature reserve on the shore of the Dead Sea, the scenery resembling biblical Eden as the icy water of **David's Spring**, fringed with green

Below: *Heat shimmers off the Dead Sea year-round.*

ferns, gushes out of the rock. Not surprisingly, **wildlife** is abundant here and you're bound to see ibex, wild sheep, and hyraxes (small rodent-like animals). Gazelles, oryx, foxes, and jackals also live here but are harder to spot, as are the 13 leopards in the reserve, which scientists have electronically tagged.

David's Spring is busy, particularly so in summer, but there's plenty of hiking amongst the rocks and canyons (remember to take lots of water with you) and in the **Nathal Arugot**, a canyon to the south of the waterfall, there are wonderfully cool rock pools where visitors routinely ignore the signs saying 'no bathing'. The reserve is open 08:00–15:30 daily.

Ein Gedi is also a good spot for the mandatory dip in the Dead Sea. Only ever swim where there are beach showers, as the crust of minerals left by the evaporating water on your skin acts as an irritant. Attempting to swim can be hilarious. Mobility is virtually impossible and you'll find your feet will keep bobbing up in front of you! Avoid tasting the water – it's foul – and don't get it in your eyes. Anyone with cuts will soon know about it as the salt creates a sharp sting. Also try digging under the sand for the famous black mud, which, when applied all over the body, is supposed to cure aches and pains.

Masada ★★★

Masada is one of the most spectacular and poignant sites in Israel. A remote table-top mountain with deep *wadis* on each side and the Dead Sea shimmering turquoise in the distance, Masada was the site of the mass suicide by the Zealots in AD73; since then it has been a symbol of national pride.

The earliest fortifications were built here in the 2nd century BC. In AD40, **King Herod** built one of his numerous impenetrable fortresses to serve as a 'bolt hole'. Later, there was a Roman garrison on Masada, but a band of 960 Zealots – men, women and children

Above: *Refreshing waterfalls turn Ein Gedi into a Garden of Eden.*

DEAD HEALTHY

'Dead' is something of a misnomer; the Dead Sea has all sorts of beneficial properties for health:
• **Skin:** The extra 400m (1300ft) that the sun's rays have to travel means relatively low levels of harmful ultraviolet radiation and many visitors to the area find their acne or psoriasis dry up but their skin doesn't burn.
• **Joints:** Mineral-rich mud helps ease rheumatic or arthritic joints, as does the sensation of weightlessness in the salty water.
• **Asthma:** The evaporating water has a high concentration of oxygen and bromide, easing allergies and asthma.

Above: *Masada's setting is hauntingly beautiful.*

SODOM AND GOMORRAH

According to the Old Testament, Sodom and Gomorrah were two ancient cities near the Dead Sea. Because of the sexual perversions of their inhabitants, the cities were destroyed by fire and brimstone and a mighty earthquake. Abraham's nephew, **Lot**, pleaded with the Lord to spare him and his family, and they were allowed to flee the destruction. But when Lot's wife turned around, she froze into a pillar of salt. A cave on the shores of the lake, its walls encrusted with salt, is said to mark the spot today.

under the leadership of Eleazarben Yair – stormed Masada in AD66 in an uprising against the Romans and took control of the mountain. Herod had filled the vast water tanks and grain stores for a potential siege and there was plenty for the Zealots to live on, even after the 10,000 Romans – who were camped round the base of the mountain – had cut off the water supply.

After three years of waiting, the Romans started to build a wall around Masada, blocking all possible escape routes, and then constructed a huge, earthern ramp reinforced by wooden beams up to the top of the mountain. They advanced up the ramp with flaming torches and battering rams and the Zealots knew the end was near. Rather than fight the Romans and die as slaves, Eleazarben decided his people should die with dignity. The men drew lots to decide who would do the deed. Each man killed his family and then himself until just 10 were left. One killed the other nine and then took his own life. Even the Romans, when they broke through the smouldering remains of the walls the next day, admitted admiration for the nobility of the Zealots, as recounted by the historian, Flavius Josephus, in his book, *The Jewish War*.

Nobody can fail to be touched by Masada, which has a gloomy air under the baking sun, even today. You can get to the top by cable car (open 08:00–16:00) or on foot, clambering up the **Snake Path** which has magnificent views, or up the **Battery**, the Romans' ramp (both are open 04:30–15:30; it's important to get to the site early in order to witness the magnificent sunrise!). Sometimes there are long queues for the cable car, but it's worth it just to stand on the top looking down at the Roman encampments and trying to imagine how the Zealots must have felt.

The excavation of Masada in the 1960s was incredibly exciting, revealing Herod's fortress and the later, the more modest accommodation of the Zealots, including their synagogue. In Herod's palace, beautiful mosaics were

uncovered revealing patterns of olive branches, vines and pomegranates. There were also highly sophisticated baths. Climb down into one of the vast water cisterns and marvel at Herod's system of diverting flood water from the *wadis* to the mountain. Masada continues to stir emotions amongst Israelis today, and a swearing-in ceremony is held here annually for young military recruits who declare: 'Masada shall not fall again'. A sound and light show tells the story of Masada. (March–August 21:00, September–October 19:00) with translations into English.

Arad ★

West from the Dead Sea, the mountain-top town of Arad, is a carefully planned 1960s town. Nearby Tel Arad, an excavated and partly reconstructed Canaanite settlement, is over 5000 years old. A second excavation has revealed a fortress from the 10th century BC, with the remains of a sanctuary modelled on the former Temple in Jerusalem. The Arad Visitors' Centre contains a display of the finds, and offers a sound and light show. Open 09:00–17:00 Monday–Friday, Sunday; 09:00–14:30 Saturday.

KIBBUTZ LIFE

No-one on a kibbutz has any money, and none ever changes hands. Everything is held in a central fund and workers can withdraw cash for 'special' items not supplied by the kibbutz if deemed important. Every night after supper there is a meeting, at which every issue from housekeeping to social issues is debated and decided upon. Children live in a separate house (originally a fortified building where they would be safe from invading Arabs) and spend just a few hours a day with their parents. Women enjoy complete equality. The work, however, is tough. On the agricultural kibbutzim, the working day begins at 04:30, with a siesta during the heat of the day. However, with the decline in agriculture and the increase in secondary and tertiary industry that comes with the developed world, the whole existence of the kibbutz in its traditional form is now under threat.

Above left: *Sections of original tiled floor still remain at Masada.*
Left: *The ruins of Masada not only bear witness to a remarkable feat of architecture, but also have their own tragic story.*

Below: *River beds in the Negev Desert make challenging hikes.*

THE NEGEV

Heading west and south from Arad, the Judean Desert becomes the vast Negev, mile upon mile of rocky desert rising into rugged mountains in the south. The Negev occupies 60% of Israel's land but is home to only 10% of its people. The desert does, however, play an important role: defence installations are hidden here; some areas are irrigated and farmed; and there's a handful of ancient sites, dating back thousands of years to when the desert was green and in bloom.

Be'er Sheva ★

The capital of the Negev region and Israel's fourth-largest town, Be'er Sheva is a big, busy industrial settlement, mainly Jewish but with a large **Bedouin** population as well. The best feature is the Thursday morning Bedouin Market on the town's southern fringe, a Middle Eastern cacophony of camel trading, goat and sheep auctions, arts and crafts, brass, leather and incense, not to mention its excellent food stalls selling sticky baklava, dripping

with honey. Not surprisingly, the market has become something of a tourist attraction.

Avdat ★★

Due south of Be'er Sheva is the ancient **Nabatean** settlement of Avdat, dating back to the second century BC. The excavations themselves, burial caves, kilns and churches, are interesting but what is

really fascinating is the reconstruction of the Nabateans' desert farms. Archaeologists and botanists have rebuilt the Nabateans' unique system of gullies and terraces which collect flash flood water after a storm, and are producing miraculous groves of apricot trees, vines and wheatfields with no additional irrigation.

Above: *Anything and everything is for sale at Be'er Sheva's market.*

Mitzpe Ramon ★★★

The desert town of Mitzpe Ramon perches on the lip of a vast crater, 40km (25 miles) long and 12km (7½ miles) wide, now designated as a national park. The crater, known as **Maktesh Ramon**, has expansive vistas across a moon-like landscape of sheer, rocky sides, and its undulating floor of dune-like hills and green *wadis*. The rock formations are rich in minerals, stained in yellow, purple and red. All sorts of fossilized remains, dating back 200 million years, have been found here.

Today, Mitzpe Ramon is an activity centre, with people **hang-gliding** off the top of the crater walls, **abseiling** down the sides and **horse-trekking** across the floor. You can also hire **camels** for a short trek along the crater rim. Despite the snorting and spitting of the camels, this is a wonderfully peaceful way to soak up the dramatic scenery. If you're travelling with children, visit the nearby **Alpaca Farm**, where llamas and alpaca can be petted.

FIRST PM OF ISRAEL

David Ben-Gurion (1886–1973) dedicated his life to establishing a Jewish homeland in Palestine. He left his native Poland in 1906 to work on a farm in a Jewish settlement in Turkish Palestine. In 1910 he became editor of the Zionist workers' newspaper, *Achdut*. In 1930 he formed the Mapai, the Zionist labour party. Throughout World War II, Ben-Gurion battled to allow Jews to immigrate to Palestine, and he became the first prime minister of the new Israel. He remained in the Knesset until his retirement from politics in 1970. For the last 10 years of his life he lived at Sede Boqer, a kibbutz in the Negev. He died here in 1973.

Above: *The bizarre Mushroom in Timna National Park.*

DONKEYS IN ISRAEL

The Asian wild ass, on which Jesus rode into Jerusalem on Palm Sunday, is slowly being reintroduced into Israel as part of the Hai-Bar programme. The ass is usually reddish-brown in colour but may also be yellowish or grey. It can reach a speed of up to 70kph (43mph), and can run at 24kph (15mph) for as long as two hours. The wild ass became extinct in Israel, having been hunted for its flesh (considered superior to venison) and for its skin, which is used to make a leather called *shagreen*. Only about 3000 individuals remain in Africa, but in Mongolia some wild herds still number as many as 1000 creatures.

Hai-Bar Nature Reserve ★★

Particularly beautiful is the **Arava Valley**, with the Negev to the west and the Edom Mountains of Jordan to the east. The mountains here are a brilliant shade of pinky-red, changing to orange and purple at sunset. Rocks have been wind-blasted into peculiar shapes and desert creatures shelter from the sun in the gullies and *wadis*.

The Hai-Bar Biblical Wildlife Reserve at **Kibbutz Samar** in Yotveta is one of the game parks in Israel where species from the time of the Bible have been reintroduced. A captive breeding programme aims eventually to release the animals into the wild. With eyes peeled, it's possible to spot wolves, hyenas, ibex, cheetahs and leopards, many of which roamed free until relatively recently; a number were killed by Bedouin who saw them as a threat to their herds. You can drive around the reserve in a car and see the other 450 resident species in the enclosed area. Open 08:30–17:00 daily in summer, 08:30–16:00 in winter.

Timna National Park ★★

About 30km (20 miles) north of Eilat is Timna National Park, which includes the 6000-year-old King Solomon's mines, once worked by the the ancient Egyptians, and later by King Solomon's slaves. Copper ore was roasted in vast ovens after being dug from underground galleries. There are also some weird rock formations, notably **Solomon's Pillars**, two huge, rose-pink rock columns, and the **Mushroom**, a boulder resting on a sandstone pillar. A full-sized model of the Tabernacle was added in 1999 complete with Ark, Golden Lampstand and Altar of Incense, while a multimedia presentation explains the exodus.You can visit the remains of the Egyptian sanctuaries where the mine workers lived, and see ancient rock carvings.

EILAT

Israel's southernmost point is crammed into a tiny strip of Red Sea beach, dedicated to sun, sea, sand and scuba. To the west is the Egyptian border post of Taba and the sandy expanse of the Sinai; to the east, the Jordanian port of Aqaba and, beyond, the rugged mountains of Saudi Arabia falling into the deep blue sea. The 'riviera' lights up at night, with distant pinpricks from four different countries reflected in the water.

Under its fun-loving veneer, **Eilat** is vital to Israel, providing access to the Red Sea. Many of the young Israelis in town are part of the Israeli Defence Force.

Eilat's past is not particularly illustrious. Moses passed through and King Solomon built a port called Etzion-geber. The Queen of Sheba quite probably landed here, followed by various invaders, among them Syrians and Edomites, wresting Eilat from one another over the years. By the time **Lawrence of Arabia** passed through en route to Jordan during World War I (1914–18), Eilat was little more than a collection of fishing shacks.

When Israel became an official nation in 1948, troops were sent quickly to defend the new country's only link to Asia, Africa and Iran – important as sources of oil. Prior to the 1967 Six-Day War, Eilat was under tremendous threat from Egypt and Jordan, but Israel's pre-emptive strike and subsequent seizing of the Sinai sent the Egyptians packing. Continued Jordanian terrorist attacks prevented any kind of tourism from developing, until veiled threats from Israel forced them to tighten up border security. Thereafter, Eilat began to boom, with hotels springing up along its North Beach, divers flocking to its spectacular underwater reefs, and sun-lovers from chilly northern Europe pouring out of charter aircraft at nearby Ovda Airport in search of winter warmth.

NOMADS OF THE DESERT

Bedouin are nomadic Arabic tribes, scattered across the mountains and deserts of the Middle East, and in Israel they inhabit the **Negev Desert**. Their homes are goatskin tents, and their lives are spent herding goats, camels and sheep. Bedouin are incredibly hospitable and should you come across a tribe, invitations will be extended to share their lamb and rice, not to mention other parts of the sheep. More and more Bedouin are being settled in houses however, and the traditional way of life is disappearing.

Below: *Sun-drenched Eilat has become a top holiday destination.*

Above: *Eilat shares in the underwater treasures of the Red Sea.*
Opposite top: *Coral World provides a glimpse of a living reef without getting wet.*

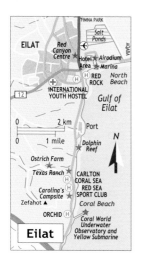

Right: *Eilat's slender strip of beach is what many visitors come for.*

North Beach **

The focal point of Eilat is North Beach, a sandy strip backed by a palm-lined promenade and a string of deluxe hotels. The town spreads back over the hills from here, although visitors need stray no further to find restaurants, nightlife and duty-free shopping. Because space on the crowded beach is limited, a lagoon has been built behind the front line of hotels so that others, too, can claim a waterfront position.

Unlike neighbouring Coral Beach, where watersports are banned to protect the shallow reefs, North Beach is not a designated national park and visitors can **swim**, **sail** and **windsurf** from the sand. Regular **boat trips** operate from the **marina** and a sunset cruise is well worth the effort to watch the incredible changing colours of the desert from the water.

Coral World ***

Down towards the Egyptian border is Coral Beach, 6km (4 miles) out of town. A couple of deluxe hotels are located here, but because the coral reefs are just a metre or so offshore, watersports are prohibited. The

Coral World Underwater Observatory, however, is outstanding and well worth a visit. The observatory is built under the water; descend the spiral staircase inside the white tower and admire the incredible marine life: corals in rainbow colours with orange, yellow, scarlet and electric-blue fish flitting by, and purple fronds waving in the gentle current. Elsewhere there are sharks and rays contained in an enclosure. Visitors who want to try snorkelling can visit the **Coral Reserve** nearby, where underwater markers take you on a trail across the reef. The Observatory is open 08:30–16:00 Saturday–Thursday, 08:30–15:30 Friday.

Yellow Submarine ★★

Next to the Coral World Observatory is the departure point for Eilat's 48-seater submarine. The submarine dives over the underwater ledge to 25m (80ft) for views of rarer species and giant coral formations; these are very exciting, especially for marine-life enthusiasts and children. Open 10:00–15:30 daily except Saturday.

PARTING OF THE SEAS

The Red Sea occupies a portion of the East African Rift Valley, a geological fault along which the earth's crust has been tearing apart for more than 50 million years. The Red Sea formed when the Arabian peninsula was torn from Africa 20 million years ago. It is 2253km (1400 miles) long, up to 2134m (7000ft) deep and just 354km (220 miles) wide at its broadest point, although geologists have found evidence on the sea floor that proves that the Red Sea is still, very slowly, getting wider. The site where the waters miraculously parted to allow the Israelites and Moses to cross is believed to be the Gulf of Suez.

Dolphin Reef ★★★

Located on South Beach, between Coral World and the hotel area of North Beach, Dolphin Reef is an area where semi-wild dolphins turn up daily to be fed. Visitors can stand on a platform to watch the dolphins appearing through an opening in the underwater nets that enclose the area. They leap out of the water and perform tricks, even though the staff insist the dolphins have not been trained. There's also no guarantee that they will come every day. For an extra fee, visitors can go snorkelling alongside the dolphins and for yet another fee (you need to book in advance), you may dive with them. Failing this, there's a pleasant café with outdoor seating and a small sandy beach for sunbathing.

Airodium ★

An ideal distraction for bored teenagers, this unusual entertainment centre allows you to experience the feeling of free fall. Visitors don a special suit and 'fly' on a strong jet of air that keeps them hovering a few metres above the ground, before letting them down gently on to a large mattress. Open 10:00–13:00 and 17:00–22:00 Monday–Saturday (summer), 10:00–18:00 in winter.

Below: *For those tempted to take up scuba diving, Eilat is a good learning ground, with plenty of training facilities on offer.*

Bird-watching ★★★

Eilat is a bird-watcher's dream since it is situated on the main migration route from Europe to North Africa. In spring and autumn, tales of sightings reach almost biblical proportions as thousands of eagles, pelicans, kites and buzzards darken the skies over Eilat.

The **Nature Reserves' Authority**, which has an office in the King Solomon Hotel, has set up special trails for bird-watchers and has also installed hidden observation points for watching the lagoon birds. There are also slide shows, lectures and nature films on offer during the migration season.

Desert Adventures ★★★

Various companies run safaris into the Negev from Eilat. These include four-wheel-drive excursions along the *wadis*, **quad-biking** along off-road trails, **horse-riding, camel trekking** and

climbing opportunities. One of the best hikes is the **Red Canyon**, accessible with a guide, where you scramble down a gorge, its rocks smoothed by water over millions of years. For part of the walk you hang on to ropes and metal footholds, while at points you can actually slide down the shiny rock on your backside!

Above: *Petra's ancient amphitheatre, carved into the rock.*
Below: *The sheer scale of the structures at Petra is breathtaking.*

EXCURSIONS BEYOND ISRAEL

Egyptian Sinai ★

Tour companies in Eilat arrange side-trips into the Egyptian Sinai to visit **St Catherine's Monastery, Mount Sinai** – where **Moses** received the **Ten Commandments** while leading the Israelites through the desert – and, for divers, the Egyptian coastal resort of **Sharm el-Sheikh**. Visitors can also cross the border (without the need for a visa) at Taba to use the beach and facilities of the Hilton.

Petra ★★★

Jordan's breathtaking 'rose-red city' is fast becoming a popular side-trip now that the Arava border post at Aqaba – a few minutes' drive from Eilat – is open. The trip is quite arduous; but the ancient capital of the Nabateans is so astonishing, carved as it is into a sheer, rose-coloured rock face at the end of a deep rock fissure, that the trip is worthwhile. Several hotels have opened recently to cater for the increasing number of tourists.

The Dead Sea and Negev at a Glance

BEST TIMES TO VISIT

Eilat is a **year-round** resort with hot, dry summers and mild winters. In summer, the resort is popular with Israelis and in winter, numerous holiday-makers arrive from northern Europe. Winter evenings are chilly, so be sure to bring warm clothes.

The **Dead Sea**, meanwhile, is perfect in **winter**, when you can experience mild, dry weather. **Spring** and **autumn** are also good times to visit. Avoid the middle of summer, though, which is punishingly hot and humid.

GETTING THERE

The **Dead Sea** lies between the **international airports** of Tel Aviv and Eilat. From Tel Aviv, the **drive** takes about 90 minutes, or alternatively you can drive from Jerusalem which takes half an hour. **Eilat** is about three hours' drive further south, or a 60-minute flight from Tel Aviv on the **Arkia** airline. Eilat itself has an international airport at Ovda, tel: (08) 634-4405, which is 40 minutes' drive away, and a domestic airport, tel: (08) 636-3808, in the middle of the town. Charter flights from all over Europe serve Ovda and El Al operates direct flights. **Egged buses** run scheduled services between Jerusalem, Tel Aviv and Eilat and there are **car rental** companies in Eilat. See *Useful Contacts* for phone numbers.

GETTING AROUND

Getting around the **Dead Sea** is possible by public bus, **hire car** or **tour bus**. Taxis, **buses** (**Egged**, tel: (03) 694-8888) and *sherut* serve the urban areas of **Eilat** and several companies in the area run 4WD excursions into the desert. Visitors should not drive off-road in the desert. Camel caravan tours allow you to see the desert at a slower pace! Regular excursions run to **Petra** in Jordan, with an Israeli bus or taxi taking you to the border and a Jordanian vehicle and guide picking you up on the Jordanian side.

WHERE TO STAY

Dead Sea
LUXURY
Hotel Le Meridien Dead Sea, Dead Sea Post 89680, tel: (07) 659-1234. Spectacular modern hotel with excellent leisure facilities and the country's best spa.
Radisson Moriah Plaza Dead Sea Spa Hotel, Dead Sea Post 86960, tel: (07) 659-1591, fax: 658-4238. Luxury hotel on the beach with spa centre.
Grand Nirvana Resort and Spa Hotel, Dead Sea Post 86930, tel: (07) 668-9444, www.nirvana.co.il Private beach and spa centre, 208-room hotel.
MID-RANGE
Ein Gedi Kibbutz Hotel, Dead Sea Post 86980, tel: (07) 659-4222, eg@ein-gedi.org.il Kibbutz with a swimming pool and sports

facilities as well as a shuttle service to the Ein Gedi Spa.
Ein Gedi Beach Holiday Village, Dead Sea Post 86980, tel: (07) 658-4342, fax: 658-4455. Bungalows and caravans, with a shuttle to Ein Gedi Spa.
BUDGET
Ein Gedi Youth Hostel, on the shores of the Dead Sea, tel: (08) 658-4165, eingedi@iyha.org.il Facilities include rooms with air conditioning, café and TV room.
Masada Youth Hostel, at the foot of Masada, tel: (08) 995-3222, massada@iyha.org.il Facilities available include rooms with air conditioning, café and a picnic area.

Eilat
Eilat hotels are big, brash and modern, so don't expect anything rustic. Most are situated in the North Beach area where the beachfront is at a premium, while lower-grade establishments are set back from the sea.
LUXURY
Eilat Princess, PO Box 2323, Eilat, tel: (07) 636-5555, sales@eilatprincess.com Beautiful hotel just outside Eilat with magnificent pool and stunning views.
Isrotel Royal Beach, PO Box 765, Eilat, tel: (07) 636-8888, royal-beach@isrotel.co.il Large resort hotel, modern luxuries, located on the North Beach.
Dan Eilat, PO Box 2122, Eilat, tel: (07) 636-2222, daneilat@

danhotels.com Modern Dan property next to the Royal Beach. Five-star luxury.

MID-RANGE

Orchid, PO Box 994, Eilat, tel: (07) 636-0360, orchid@net vision.net.il This is an unusual Thai-style development, near the Coral Reef Observatory. It offers comfortable bungalow accommodation.

Red Sea Sport Club Hotel, PO Box 390, Eilat, tel: (07) 637-2171, www.redseasports.co.il Low-rise hotel with pleasant pool, set slightly inland.

BUDGET

International Youth Hostel, Arava Road, Eilat, tel: (07) 637-0088, eilat@iyha.org.il Located in town, one block back from the beach. Facilities include a shop, TV room, rooms with air conditioning and a café.

WHERE TO EAT

You will find that there is very little tourist infrastructure along the Dead Sea; therefore most restaurants are located in hotels and *kibbutzim*. Day-trippers can eat lunch at the hotels – the Moriah Plaza does a particularly good buffet. In Eilat everything from pizza to pancakes, French to Thai cuisine, is available, often with live entertainment.

Eilat

The Blue Fish, Bell Hotel, tel: (07) 633-7450. Fish, seafood, French cuisine and meat dishes.

La Coquille, tel: (07) 637-3461. Expensive but good French cuisine.
Country Chicken, tel: (07) 637-1312. Good, basic Jewish cooking.
Red Sea Star, tel: (07) 634-7777. Fantastic aquatic theme restaurant 5m (16ft) below the water level.

SHOPPING

Eilat is a duty-free zone and has great shopping buys such as perfume, jewellery and electronic goods. Shopping in the Dead Sea area is limited, though the Dead Sea beauty products are of excellent quality, available from the spas. The best market in the region is the Bedouin Market in Be'er Sheva on Thursday.

TOURS AND EXCURSIONS

Tour companies based in Eilat include **Egged**, tel: (07) 373-148; **Galilee Tours**, tel: (08) 633-5131; **Johnny Desert Tours**, tel: (07) 632-5265. Trips operate to the Dead Sea and Masada, and to Jerusalem. Various 4WD tours operate into the desert, usually including hiking and camel riding. Try **Walkways**,

tel: (02) 534-4452, rockman@ netvision.net.il All the tour operators sell trips to Petra in Jordan, using Jordanian buses and guides from the Jordanian side of the Arava border crossing, outside Eilat.
Scuba diving: Aqua Sport, Coral Beach, tel: (07) 633-4404; Lucky Divers, Red Sea Tower, tel: (07) 633-5990; Dolphin Reef, tel: (07) 637-6787 (telephone the Dolphin Reef several weeks in advance to book a dive with dolphins).
Masada Sound and Light Show, tel: (07) 995-9333.

USEFUL CONTACTS

Dead Sea Tourist Information Office, tel: (07) 668-8808.
Qumran Visitors Centre, tel: (02) 993-6330, fax: (02) 994-2533.
Arad Tourist Information Office, tel: (07) 995-4409.
Eilat Tourist Centre, tel: (07) 637-2111.
Eilat Bird-watching Park, tel: (07) 633-5319.
Car rental companies in Eilat include:
Avis, tel: (08) 637-3164; Budget, tel: 08701 539170; Hertz, tel: (08) 637-5050.

EILAT	J	F	M	A	M	J	J	A	S	O	N	D
AVERAGE TEMP. °F	59	63	68	77	79	88	90	91	88	79	72	63
AVERAGE TEMP. °C	15	17	20	25	26	31	32	33	31	26	22	17
Hours of sun daily	7	8	8	9	10	11	11	11	10	9	8	7
RAINFALL in	0	.31	.31	.19	0	0	0	0	0	0	0	.31
RAINFALL mm	0	8	8	5	0	0	0	0	0	0	0	8
Days of rainfall	0	6	6	3	0	0	0	0	0	0	0	7

6
Galilee

A far cry from the stony Negev or the stark mountains around the Dead Sea, Galilee is composed of green, rolling hills, with the snowy cap of **Mount Hermon** in the distance, the whole juxtaposed against the shimmering blue of the **Sea of Galilee**. Israel's beautiful north is a place to refresh mind, body and soul.

Just 157km (97 miles) from Jerusalem, Galilee is a popular summer holiday centre for Israelis, despite the humidity. The area is also of deep importance to Christians, who flock to the sites where Jesus is said to have performed eight miracles, to see his home town of **Nazareth**, to visit the holy **Mount Tabor**, and to be baptized in the **River Jordan**.

Jews, meanwhile, visit **Safed**, a beautiful old town in the hills – much of it unchanged since the 16th century – and site of the tombs of many important Jewish scholars. Bird-watchers descend on the **Hula Valley** to study the spectacular annual migration, whilst adventurers take to the skies in hang-gliders, to the saddle for leisurely trekking or to the foaming waters of the river in inflatable rafts.

Galilee's main holiday centre is the lakeside town of **Tiberias**, famous for its curative **hot springs**. In addition to hotels and holiday villages, there are several excellent **kibbutzim** around the lake which accept visitors. In winter there's a **ski resort** on Mount Hermon, part of the range that forms the brooding mass of the **Golan Heights**, the buffer zone between Israel and neighbouring Syria.

DON'T MISS

★★★ Beit She'an: explore the Roman excavations.
★★★ Ancient biblical sites: drive round the lake and visit fascinating biblical sites.
★★ Jordan River Park: river rafting and kayaking are on offer for the adventurous.
★★ Capernaum: discover the place where Jesus did much of his preaching.
★ Banias: hike in the Golan Heights.
★ Vered Hagalil Ranch: enjoy the pleasures of horse-riding here.

Opposite: *Tiberias is now a thriving resort on the Sea of Galilee.*

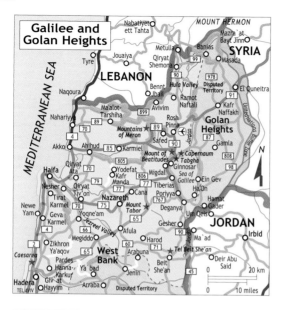

Galilee and Golan Heights

TIBERIAS

On the surface, Tiberias is a fun-loving resort, spread out along the banks of the lake, its promenade lined with outdoor fish restaurants and its marina packed with pleasure cruisers. This is, however, one of Israel's four Jewish holy cities, along with **Safed**, **Jerusalem** and **Hebron**, and several important Jewish scholars are buried here, among them the 12th-century philosopher Moses Maimonides.

Tiberias was founded by Herod the Great's son, Herod Antipas, in AD20 and by the seventh century had become a thriving academic centre. Battling Muslims and Crusaders largely destroyed it in the 12th century and a massive earthquake in 1837 finished off the remainder of the ancient buildings. Consequently, Tiberias is now very much a modern resort with a few crumbling remains scattered around.

SEA OF KINNERET

The Sea of Galilee was once part of a great inland sea extending from the Hula marshes in northern Israel to a point some 64km (40 miles) south of the Dead Sea. The lake is encircled by sandy beaches and bordered by escarpments on the east and southwest and by plains on the north and northwest. The water is cool and clear and contains many species of fish, notably sardines and tilapia, which are sold in the many fish restaurants around the lake. The grebe, gull, pelican, and other species of birds are abundant while animal life includes tortoise, turtle, crayfish and a small crustacean known as the beach flea.

Things to see include the old city walls, best preserved near the Moriah Plaza Hotel, and the artists' studios at the **Donna Gracia** complex, a former citadel in the northwest corner of town. Tombs include those of **Moses Maimonides** and of the great Jewish thinker **Rabbi Akiva**, who was executed by the Romans in AD135.

It's also worth getting up at dawn, when the lake is usually like a sheet of glass, and watching the fishing boats bringing back their haul, just as they did in ancient biblical times.

Tiberias Hot Springs ★★

Built on the lake shore, this spa complex covers a fault that has caused 17 hot, sulphuric springs to gush up from 1081m (6500ft) below the earth's crust at temperatures of up to 60°C (140°F). There are thermal pools, mud wraps, massage, hydrotherapy and Jacuzzi baths for visitors to enjoy, despite the rather pungent smell in the air of sulphuric gases. The ruins of an ancient Jewish city, **Hammath Tiberias**, were discovered next to the springs and include exquisite mosaics among the remains of a 4th-century synagogue. Tel: (04) 672-8500.

Above and opposite:
Fishing boats set out at dawn; the St Peter fish is a common catch.

MAN OF LETTERS

Moses Maimonides was born in Spain in 1135 and was a leading sage of his time. He studied medicine in Cairo and became a leading court physician. His greatest achievement was the writing of the *Mishnah Torah*, a document which simplified the whole of Jewish teaching and belief from the *Talmud*. He also wrote the *Guide of the Perplexed*, a presentation of the philosophy of Judaism. He was buried in Tiberias in 1204 and his tomb on Rabbi Abulafiya Street is an important pilgrimage site.

MIRACLES OF GALILEE

Many significant episodes from the **New Testament** happened in the Galilee region. They include:
• The Annunciation – when the Angel told Mary of Nazareth that she would bear the Son of God.
• The miracle of turning water into wine.
• The feeding of the 5000.
• The miracle of walking on the water.
• The miracle of the Gaderene Swine.
• The Transfiguration – when the prophets Moses and Elijah appeared to Jesus and his disciples on Mount Tabor.

AROUND THE LAKE

The Sea of Galilee is surprisingly small – just 50km (36 miles) in circumference. A good road runs right round the lake, hugging the shore and passing through various points of interest. Even if you don't stop much, the scenery is stunning and the countryside unspoilt. In summer the weather is very humid (the lake is actually 120m, or 390ft, below sea level) and there are plenty of swimming places. Spend the day at a leisurely pace and remember to try the delicious St Peter's fish, a freshwater species from the lake named, of course, after St Peter, one of the apostles.

There are several ways to get around the lake: by **car**; by **bicycle**, which can be hired in Tiberias; by **foot**, stopping for the night in one of the kibbutzim along the way; or on the special **Egged bus service** which has an all-day ticket, the Minus 200, allowing you to get on and off as you please at the 23 stops. **Ferries** also travel across the lake to **Ein Gev** on the east coast, a route serious swimmers attempt once a year in a challenge race.

Heading north from Tiberias, the road looks down on the dazzling white rooftops of **Migdal**, birthplace of Mary Magdalene. Just beyond here is the **Kibbutz Ginnosar**, which harbours an amazing find: an old fishing boat, discovered in the mud at the bottom of the lake when the water was low. The boat has been dated as 2000 years old, so would probably have been in use during the time of Jesus.

Below: *Roman baths at Hamat Gader are a great source of mineral-rich, beautifying mud.*

A little further on at **Tabgha** is a Byzantine-style basilica, the **Church of the Multiplication**, built in 1981 (incorporating its 5th-century predecessor) with beautiful mosaic floors depicting flora and birds. At the front of the altar is a mosaic of the loaves and fishes, alluding to the biblical story of the feeding of the 5000. Open 08:30–17:00 Monday–Saturday; 09:30–17:00 Sunday.

From here, follow the signs to the **Mount of Beatitudes**, where an Italian church (dating back to 1937) marks the spot of the Sermon on the Mount. Open 08:00–12:00, 14:30–17:00 daily.

At the northern end of the lake, **Capernaum** is the ancient town where Jesus did much of his preaching. Several of his disciples, including Peter, are believed to have come from here. In AD700 the town was destroyed after the Arab conquest. However, there are two excavated sites worth visiting: **St Peter's House**, and next to it, a 1700-year-old synagogue. Open 08:30–16:15 daily.

Above: *Pilgrims come from around the world to be baptized in the River Jordan.*

The eastern side of the lake is much less developed, with a string of sandy beaches and a few holiday villages. You can stop and swim or rent a boat at the **Kibbutz Ein Gev**, about halfway down. A short detour towards the Jordanian border leads to **Hamat Gader**, another hot spring, which has remained popular since Roman times. The spring has been channelled into a pool and there's plenty of black mud which is reputed to be very beneficial for your skin. Also of interest here are some impressive Roman ruins and an amphitheatre, and if you're trailing fractious children around the historic sites, there is the unexpected treat of an alligator farm! As an added bonus, the **Kibbutz Ha'On** on the lake shore has an ostrich farm.

On the southwestern shore, at the point where the River Jordan leaves the lake, is the spot where John the Baptist is believed to have baptized Jesus so that he could set out on his mission. Now there's a specially constructed baptismal site here where white-robed pilgrims line up to be submerged in the water in order to be spiritually 'cleansed'.

SAINT MARY

Mary Magdalene was born in Migdal on the shores of the Sea of Galilee. She is thought to have been a prostitute and is referred to in the Bible as a 'sinning woman'. Jesus healed her of evil spirits and she became a devout follower, anointing his feet and keeping a vigil at the foot of the cross during the crucifixion. It was to Mary Magdalene that Jesus appeared after his resurrection. She is remembered as a saint and her feast day on the Christian calendar is July 22.

Above: *Nazareth, once a tiny village, is a sprawling town nowadays.*

NAZARETH

Once a tiny, rustic village, Nazareth comes as something of a surprise. It is now a slightly unattractive, sprawling town, with a large Christian Arab population living mainly in the old area, and a modern sec-tion, **Natzeret Illit**, populated by Jews. Nazareth was the home of the Holy Family, and churches, basilicas and convents have sprung up everywhere to commemorate even the most minor happenings. The town is an essential pilgrimage for Christians and is always busy with tour buses.

Basilica of the Annunciation ★★

A modern, imposing church built in 1966, this basilica covers the spot where Mary's house would have stood, and on which Byzantine and Crusader churches were built. Its unusual dome dominates the skyline of Nazareth. Inside, brightly coloured murals from different countries depict the Annunciation. Stroll from here down Pilgrim's Walk, created for the Millennium celebrations, to Mary's Well, site of Mary's first encounter with the Archangel Gabriel. Open 08:30–11:45, 14:00–16:45 daily.

St Joseph's Church ★

Across the square is the more modest St Joseph's Church, built over a cavern which is believed to have been Joseph's carpentry workshop. Opening times as above.

St Gabriel Greek Orthodox Church ★★

Up the hill heading out of town is the spot where Greek Orthodox belief has it that the Angel Gabriel appeared to Mary whilst she was fetching water. The 17th-century church – which is ornate inside, and covers ancient stones remaining from three earlier churches – is built over an underground spring. The spring is connected by a subterranean aqueduct to Mary's Well, believed to contain water with curative properties. Open 08:30–12:00 and 14:00–17:45 (until 16:30 in winter) Monday– Saturday. Open Sunday for mass.

Cana ★

A few miles north of Nazareth is Cana, where Jesus is supposed to have performed his first miracle – that of turning water into wine. The village today, surrounded by pomegranate groves, is populated by Arabs; it has two churches, a Franciscan and a Greek Orthodox Church, both marking the supposed site of the miracle. Cana is easily accessible from Nazareth and a bus runs every 45 minutes.

THE JEZREEL VALLEY

With a car, it's possible to make a leisurely meander around the lush and rather dramatic-looking Jezreel Valley. The road climbs up **Mount Tabor** and winds down again to dramatic Roman remains in **Beit She'an**, from where you can head back up the Jordan River Valley to Tiberias.

Mount Tabor ★★

Mount Tabor, 18km (11 miles) southwest of **Tiberias**, has been an important religious site since the Canaanites first inhabited this area. Sacrifices were performed here and an ancient shrine to the pagan god, Baal, can still be seen in the rock face below the **Church of the Transfiguration**, high up on the mountain. The Canaanites were defeated by the prophet Deborah, according to the *Book of Judges*, who led an army of 10,000 Israelites to victory on this mountain.

According to a 4th-century interpretation of the *Book of Luke*, Mount Tabor is where the **Transfiguration** took place. Here Jesus appeared to the apostles, transfigured, his garments a dazzling white, as he spoke to the prophets Moses and Elijah.

If it's not too hot, walk up the 3km (2-mile) dirt road to the beautiful **Church of the Transfiguration** built in 1924. Open 08:00–12:00, 15:00–sunset. The views down over the valley are stunning and inside the church is an interesting gold mosaic of the Transfiguration. Nearby, there's a ruined Arab castle, dating back to the 13th century.

GAN HASHLOSHA NATIONAL PARK

In the Beit She'an Valley is Gan Hashlosha (or Sachne, Arabic for 'warm'), a beautifully landscaped area with a natural swimming pool fed by springs as its central feature. The springs keep the water at 28°C (82°F) so it's great for a swim even in winter. The pool is divided by gentle waterfalls, ideal for splashing around in and safe for children. A snack bar and changing room are on site. Open 08:00–17:00 (Apr–Sep), 08:00–16:00 (Oct–Mar).

Below: *Exquisite colours in the Basilica of the Annunciation in Nazareth.*

Above: *Visitors can wander among the excavations at Tel Beit She'an; an earthquake in AD 749 is thought to have led to the collapse of columns on the main avenue.*

Tel Beit She'an ★★

Following the Jezreel Valley to the east you reach the spectacular Roman remains of Tel Beit She'an, rivalling Caesarea in magnitude. A huge **Roman amphitheatre** has been excavated, as well as a gymnasium, a theatre seating 6000, a temple and a broad avenue, or *cardo*, lined with columns believed to have toppled in an earthquake in AD749. The city is still being excavated. Open 08:00–17:00 (until 16:00 in winter) Sunday–Thursday and Saturday; 08:00–16:00 (until 15:00 in winter) Friday.

SAFED

Charming and atmospheric, the ancient hill town of Safed nestles in front of the **Mountains of Meron**. One of the four Jewish holy cities, Safed has great religious significance and attracts many visitors. Although Safed doesn't appear in the Bible, it contains the tomb of Rabbi Shimon Bar-Yochai who in the second century wrote the *Cabala*, an ancient text of Judaism. The *Schulchan Aroch*, a set of rules by which Jews live their daily lives, was later written here.

Safed enhanced its position as a seat of learning in the 16th century as thousands of intellectual Spanish Jews fleeing the Inquisition settled here. Schools and synagogues prospered until an earthquake in 1759 destroyed most of the buildings. The town only came back to life with the arrival of a large group of **Hassidim** from Eastern Europe, the descendants of whom live here today in the belief that the Messiah will descend from the Mountains of Meron to Safed before making an appearance in Jerusalem.

The unspoilt scenery and clear air have attracted many artists, who inhabit a maze of narrow lanes (known as the **Artists' Quarter**) at the bottom of the hill. Some good bargains are to be had here, once you've sifted through the tourist trash. In the same area a museum, the **Zvi Assaf Printing Museum**, houses Israel's first printing press. Afterwards, wander through the **Old Town** and peep into the many synagogues and the **Ethiopian Folk Art Centre**.

GOLAN HEIGHTS

A massive slab of uplifted basalt, the Golan Heights form the strategically vital northeast corner of Israel, Lebanon and Syria and remain a huge stumbling block in the Israel–Syria peace talks. The national parks are safe for visitors but some of the remote mountainous areas still contain land mines: hike only with a guide.

Gamla ★

A few kilometres northeast of the **Sea of Galilee**, the town of Gamla experienced a tragic repetition of Masada, during the same revolt against the Romans in AD66. Over 9000 Zealots died. Some 4000 were killed by advancing Roman troops and after a long siege, the remaining 5000 committed suicide by jumping off the jagged cliffs to their death. The Romans destroyed the town but archaeologists discovered its remains in 1968 and visitors can wander around the eerie excavations, while a colony of massive griffon vultures wheels overhead.

Banias ★★

The springs and waterfalls at Banias in the far north, one of the main sources of the River Jordan, have been worshipped since long before biblical times, when gods were believed to dwell in trees, rivers and rocks. Primitive shrines have been hollowed out of the rock, once probably containing effigies of the Greek God Pan whose name Banias derives. Muslims later associated the place with Elijah. Today, it is a national park with well-marked hiking trails. Open 08:00–17:00 in winter; 08:00–18:00 in summer.

> ### SKIING ON MOUNT HERMON
>
> Mount Hermon is somehow an unlikely place to find a **ski resort**, if one considers that it looks down over the Golan Heights to the Sea of Galilee. For experienced skiers it is only really worth a visit for its novelty value. You can ski from December to April from the Moshar Neve Ativ village. Equipment can be hired at the resort and there are runs for all standards of skier but the snow is invariably slushy. Open 08:30–15:30.

Below: To many just a place in the news, the Golan Heights are startlingly beautiful.

Galilee at a Glance

The Sea of Galilee is below sea level and, though not as low as the Dead Sea, it does get very humid in summer. This does not, however, deter Israelis from flocking to its shores and beaches. **Spring** is a lovely time of year to visit, when the hills are green and the wild flowers are out. **Autumn**, from the end of September onwards, is more tolerable for hiking in the Golan Heights and for riding holidays. Winter is cooler and more temperate and there is skiing on Mount Hermon for a very limited season.

Israel is small and Galilee is easily accessible by **road** from Jerusalem, Tel Aviv and Haifa. There are no trains or international airports here but Egged **buses** run between all the towns. There are bus stations in Tiberias, tel: (06) 679-1080; Nazareth, tel: (04) 654-9555; and Safed, tel: (06) 692-1122. **Domestic flights** operate to Rosh Pina Airport, tel: (06) 695-9901, fax: 699-0525.

Several **car hire** companies have offices in Tiberias and Nazareth. Alternatively, **mountain bikes** are available from Nachshol in Tiberias, tel: (06) 693-1864. A road runs right round the lake and there are plenty of trails in the hills and alongside the Hula

Valley. **Taxis** and *sherut* are available in Tiberias, Nazareth and Safed, where a private service operates, tel: (06) 697-0707. Alternatively, one could take the return **ferry** from Kibbutz Ein Gev to Tiberias.

The most luxurious hotels are in **Tiberias**, a bustling resort. For something different, try one of the kibbutz hotels which are reasonable, quite luxurious in some cases and a good introduction to kibbutz life.

Tiberias
LUXURY
Club Hotel, Ed Ha'am Street, Tiberias, tel: (04) 672-8000, fax: 672-3664. Large, all-suite hotel on cliff overlooking the lake. All facilities, including entertainment programme.
Gai Beach, Derech Hamer-chatzaot Street, Tiberias, tel: (04) 670-0700, fax: 679-2776.
Lively beach hotel on lake shore with 120 rooms and incorporating fun water park.
Holiday Inn, HaBanim Street, Tiberias, tel: (03) 539-0808. Spa resort including the Tiberias hot springs. Horse-riding, tennis and beach facilities are all within walking distance.
Sheraton Moriah Tiberius, HaBanim Street, Tiberias, tel: (04) 671-3333, fax: 679-2320. Large, modern hotel, part of the Radisson chain.

Convenient for all facilities in Tiberias.

MID-RANGE
Hotel Eden, 4 Ohel Ya'akov Street, Tiberias, tel: (04) 679-0070, fax: 672-2461, www.edenhotel.co.il Quiet, modern hotel in the town centre, walking distance from the beach.
Maagan, Jordan Valley 15150, tel: (04) 665-4411. Peaceful kibbutz-run holiday village on lake shore.
Ron Beach Hotel, G'dud Barak Street, Tiberias 14101, tel: (04) 679-1350, fax: 679-1351. Low-rise beach hotel north of Tiberias with café, restaurant, pool and bar.

BUDGET
Tiberias Meyouchas, 2 Jordan Street, Tiberias, tel: (04) 672-1775, fax: 672-0372. Youth hostel surrounded by gardens in central Tiberias.

Outside Tiberias
MID-RANGE
Vered Hagalil, MP Korazim 12340, tel: (04) 693-5785, fax: 693-4964.
A delightful ranch in a beautiful setting overlooking the lake. Western-style riding lessons and rides out, including overnight horseback safaris.

Upper Galilee
MID-RANGE
Kfar Blum Kibbutz Hotel, Upper Galilee 12150,

tel: (04) 683-6611.
A peaceful and surprisingly luxurious kibbutz situated in the Hula Valley. Private facilities, such as bathrooms, in all rooms and a huge swimming pool.

BUDGET
Hagoshrim Kibbutz Resort Hotel, Upper Galilee, tel: (04) 681-6000, www.hagoshrim-hotel.co.il Kibbutz hotel with views of Mount Hermon and the Golan Heights.

Tiberias is packed with restaurants ranging from South American to Italian. Open-air fish restaurants line the lake shore; don't miss the St Peter fish, which is caught in the lake and is very tasty.

Tiberias
LUXURY
Pagoda, Tiberias lake shore, tel: (04) 672-5513. Superb Thai/Chinese restaurant with outdoor seating overlooking the lake. Very popular. Owners also operate lake dinner cruises, some with dancing.

MID-RANGE
Vered Hagalil (see *Where to Stay*). Steak and local special-ities in rustic setting with views of the lake.
Spaghettini, Hotel Galai Kinneret, Tiberias, tel: (04)

679-2331. Homemade pasta, fish and dairy specialities.

Hula Valley
BUDGET
Dan-Trout Restaurant, Kiriat Shmonah, Hula Valley, tel: (04) 695-0225. Working trout farm at Lake Hula.

The best shopping is in Tiberias, which is good for clothes, shoes and souvenirs, including special plastic bottles that you can fill with Jordan River water.
At the **Golan Heights Winery** in Katzrin, there are tours and tastings, tel: (04) 696-8409. For the best art galleries, spend time browsing in Safed.

Galilee is an adventure-lover's paradise, with riding, rafting, kayaking, abseiling, gliding and 4WD adventures all on offer. The **Jordan River Park** north of the lake is great for families and has picnic areas, gentle kayaking and inner tubing down the river. In winter there's skiing on Mount Hermon and in spring and autumn, bird-watching in the Hula Valley. Several companies arrange off-the-beaten-track 4WD excursions, such as the **Bat Ya'ar**, tel: (04) 692-1788. Also within easy reach of Galilee is the vast archaeo-

logical site of Beit She'an, tel: (04) 658-7189.
Nimrod's Fortress in the Golan Heights, tel: (04) 694-2360. Conventional coach tours of the biblical sites are run by **Egged**.
All terrain tours are run by **Tour Golan**, tel: (04) 696-1511.
Jordan River Rafting: white-water rafting, not operating in winter, tel: (04) 693-4622.
Horse-riding: Western-style lessons and hacks as well as overnight camping safaris on horseback; Vered Hagalil, tel: (04) 693-5785.
Mount Hermon Ski Resort, tel: (06) 698-1337. Low altitude skiing in winter.
Gliding, Mahanayim Airport, tel: (04) 693-9148. Lessons and facilities for pilots.
Abseiling, tel: (04) 690-5830.
Candle lighting at Kurs: light your own candle or have one lit for you, tel: (03) 576-6888, fax: (03) 613-2656.
Baptism at Fardenit: in the River Jordan, tel: (03) 559-6484, fax: (03) 559-6483.

Tourist information, tel: (04) 692-7845.
Kfar Blum, Jordan River Park, kayaks and inner tubes for rent, tel: (04) 690-2616.
Car rental: Budget, Elhadif Street, tel: (04) 672-0864; Eldan, tel. (03) 565-4545.

7
Haifa

Clinging to the side of **Mount Carmel** and spreading out around the busy port below, Haifa is Israel's third-largest city. From the sea, the mountain provides a stunning backdrop, thick with bottle-green pines and elegant cypresses, while the golden dome of Haifa's **Baha'i Shrine** gleams in the sunlight, and elegant homes and villas nestle between the trees.

Haifa has always been a safe haven for passing ships and it had a thriving Jewish community in the 11th century. However, it only become commercially important when the Ottoman Turks built the Hijaz railway between Damascus and Medina in 1905. The British constructed the harbour in 1934 and Haifa began to expand as it attracted more heavy industry. Today it's a centre for oil, chemicals, manufacturing and electronics, while Israel's premier Institute of Technology, HaTechnion, sprawls across the Carmel hills. Haifa residents are fond of saying that 'Jerusalem prays, Tel Aviv parties and Haifa works' and there is indeed a bustling, businesslike atmosphere.

For visitors there are long, white sandy beaches, shady parks and gardens, interesting museums, religious sites and much walking or scrambling up and down Haifa's legendary stair paths.

Out of town, there's the lush, green expanse of **Carmel Park**, several fascinating **Druze Villages** to explore, and the magnificent remains at **Akko**, one of the oldest cities in the world. Further to the south are the carefully preserved **Roman remains** at Caesarea, perhaps Israel's most beautiful archaeological site.

DON'T MISS

*** The Baha'i Shrine: explore this beautiful building with its spectacular gardens.
*** Akko: absorb its amazing Crusader heritage.
*** Caesarea: easy day trip, stunning Roman remains.
** Carmel Centre: visit this centre for its shopping, dining and sweeping views.
** Druze Villages: enjoy their handicraft shopping.
** The Thousand Step Paths: a scenic way to see the city on foot.

Opposite: *One of Haifa's highlights is the Baha'i Shrine.*

COLOUR-CODED STAIRS

Haifa has four 'Thousand Stair Paths' – and yes, each has over 1000 stairs. The colour-coded paths descend through leafy neighbourhoods, hidden alleyways and perfumed markets. The four are: the **yellow** route to the German Colony; the **red** route through Wadi Nis Nas, the Arab Quarter; the **blue** route to Paris Square in the Old City; and the **green** route, also to the Old City. All four are marked on the tourist board maps.

HAIFA

Haifa is divided into three distinct areas: the **port and industrial zone**; **Mount Carmel**, the main centre of culture and entertainment; and **Hadar HaCarmel**, the business and commercial centre.

Baha'i Shrine ★★★

Haifa is known for its religious tolerance and is a fitting location for the world headquarters of the Baha'i faith, which preaches the unity of all world religions and believes that Moses, Jesus, Buddha and Mohammed were all fundamentally bearers of the same message. The faith has some four million followers worldwide.

Baha'i was founded in Persia and its leader, the prophet known as El Bab, was executed there for

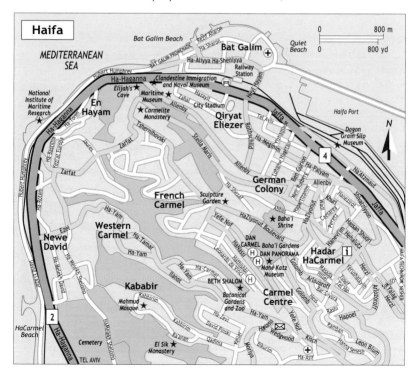

heretical preachings in 1850. His remains are kept in the Haifa mausoleum, now a centre of pilgrimage for all Baha'i followers. Bab's successor, Mirza Hussein Ali, or Baha 'u'llah, after whom the religion was named, is buried in the gardens in nearby **Akko**, the direction in which **Bab's shrine** on the hill faces.

The shrine itself is magnificent, and the carefully manicured gardens a wonderfully shady place to rest. The gardens have recently been extended to stretch from the mountain top to the seafront. The shrine is open from 09:00–12:00 daily. The gardens are open 09:00–17:00 daily except Friday and Saturday.

Above: *The shrine of the prophet El Bab is a centre of pilgrimage.*

Sculpture Garden ★

Further up the hillside along **HaZiyonut Boulevard**, which twists its way across the mountain, is a beautiful sculpture garden containing more than 20 impressive bronze sculptures by Ursula Malbin. The garden has magnificent views of the coast, the northern mountains towards the Lebanese border and the bustling port below.

HaTechnion ★

In the same direction is the Technion, Israel's Institute of Technology, spread across a 120ha (296-acre) campus on the mountain top. A visitor centre shows a short film about the Institute's research at 09:00, 11:00 and 13:00. Open 08:00–14:00 Sunday–Thursday; 08:00–12:00 Friday.

Carmel Centre ★★★

Carmel Centre, on top of the mountain, is considered prime real estate with its shady trees and breathtaking views. Most of the big hotels and fashionable shops are along **HaNassi Avenue**, lined with restaurants and pavement cafés. From Derekh Ha-Yam Street, there's a short footpath, **Nahal Lotem**, which follows a *wadi* and has occasionally stunning views down over the city.

BAB AND THE BAHA'I

Baha'i is one of the world's fastest-growing religions. The world's five million followers live in 120,000 locations in 233 countries and encompass 2100 ethnic and tribal groups. Their belief is that there is only one God and that all the world's religions have been the various stages of his revelation to mankind. Baha'i principles include: the elimination of prejudice, equality between the sexes, the elimination of extremes of poverty and wealth, universal education, and the harmony of science and religion. Haifa's Shrine of the Bab, the faith's founder, is one of the holiest places in the Baha'i world.

HAIFA NIGHTLIFE

Haifa is a lively city and a thriving café society. Coffee shops all over the city serve delicious pastries and there are several bars and discos. Kapulsky in the Panorama Centre is a good coffee shop, while Café Neto in Carmel Centre is popular with 20-somethings. Hasandak, located in the port area, is reckoned to be one of the best bars, while Cellar Ken and Fever are popular clubs, especially among students. There are also three performing arts venues and the Cinémathèque, which shows films in English.

Stella Maris ★★

The mountain levels off into a north-facing promontory. At the top is the **French Carmelite Monastery**, established during the Third Crusade by a monastic and devout group of Crusaders. The monastery served as a hospital for Napoleon's troops during his unsuccessful siege of Akko against the Turks in 1799.

The nearby **Stella Maris Church**, dating from 1836, has beautiful, marble-covered walls and a gold dome adorned with biblical scenes, including one where the prophet, Elijah, is seen rising to Heaven. Its altar is situated directly over a small, rocky grotto which is believed by the Carmelites to have been the temporary home of Elijah. Open 08:30–13:30, 15:00–18:00 daily.

Elijah's Cave ★

Confusingly, there's another cave at the base of the cliff where Elijah is believed to have hidden on his flight from the evil King Ahab and his wife Jezebel. Furthermore, another legend states that the Holy Family took refuge in this cave on their return from Egypt, although the likelihood of the same cave being the site of two such important events hundreds of years apart (when there are plenty of other caves) is slim. Nonetheless Druze, Christians, Muslims and Jews all consider this a holy spot and pilgrims have left their mark on the stone walls. Open 08:00–17:00 Sunday–Thursday; 08:00–12:45 Friday.

Below: *Haifa has always been a safe haven for ships; in 1934 the British constructed the harbour which today serves the city's thriving industries.*

Carmel by Cable Car ★★

A bubble-like cable car, giving a recorded commentary on board, ferries visitors between **Stella Maris** and **Bat Galim**, the seafront promenade. Needless to say, the views are stunning day and night, and the cable car is popular with locals in the evenings. Open 09:00–14:00 Sunday–Thursday in winter; 09:00–18:00 Sunday–Thursday and Saturday in summer, 09:00–14:00 Fridays.

Naval Museum ★★

Near the bottom terminal of the cable car is a ship, the *Af-Al-Pi*, which means 'in spite of', commemorating the constant struggle to get illegal Jewish immigrants into Palestine under British rule, as Nazi fervour was stirred up in Europe during the 1930s and '40s. The *Af-Al-Pi* was one of the few ships that made it. The nearby Clandestine Immigration and Naval Museum shows some of the clever but often futile ways immigrants tried to enter the country and has an atmosphere of struggle and despair similar to the Checkpoint Charlie Museum in Berlin. Open 08:30–16:00 Sunday–Thursday.

Above: *Green Carmel Park provides a great escape from the bustle of the city.*

Dagon Grain Silo ★

Heading east, you will find this unusual **museum** in the industrial port area, on Ha'Atzmaut Street. It looks like a windowless apartment block but is in fact a working grain silo and museum. Murals, mosaics and old photographs explain the history of bread- and beer-making, with ancient implements and earthenware jars on display. It is open at 10:30 daily for a guided tour or by appointment.

Carmel Park ★★

Carmel Park, 8093ha (20,000 acres) of green space, hiking trails and picnic grounds, is the city's playground, peppered with pretty villages, caves, old settlements and magnificent views of the coast. The air is scented with pine, eucalyptus and cypress, and on a hot day the park is a great escape from the city.

PREHISTORIC MAN RECREATED

A good day out for all the family is a visit to the **Nahal Hame'arot Caves** at Carmel, about 3km (2 miles) south of Ein Harod. The life of prehistoric man is recreated in a suitable cave setting through an audiovisual presentation and a film. Children can have a go at reconstructing the tools used by prehistoric man. Tours in English are available. Open 08:00–16:00 Monday–Thursday, Saturday; 08:00–13:00 Friday.

Druze Villages

Isfiya and **Daliat al Carmel**, some 16km (10 miles) southeast of the Mount Carmel ridge, are two villages inhabited by the Druze religious sect. Daliat al Carmel has a great **handicraft market** every day except Friday (the Druze Shabbat) and makes an interesting stop for shopping and browsing for copperware and basketry.

Akko

Jutting out into the northern end of the **Bay of Haifa**, Akko is known for its amazing 12th-century **fortified city** built by the Crusaders. Akko's domes, minarets and solid-looking walls have seen their share of action. First a Phoenician port, Akko fell to the Arabs in 636 and became an Arab colony. The Crusaders later made Akko their principal port, but in 1291 the Mamelukes took the town. In 1749 a Bedouin sheik set up his own independent fiefdom here and set about restoring the city. He built the White Market, installed access roads and rebuilt the port and city walls. In 1799, the pasha of Akko, Ahmed Al-Jazzar, added fortifications to the city after holding off Napoleon, whose dreams of an empire in the East thereafter dissolved. In 1917 Akko was captured by Britain, but with Israel's independence in 1948, it was taken over by the Jews.

Visitors can admire the sites, take a boat around the ancient harbour to see the dense walls, and wander through the noisy, narrow streets of the *souq*. Several fish restaurants have fine views across the harbour.

Mosque of Al-Jazzar ★★

Israel's third-largest mosque, the green-domed Al-Jazzar, was built in 1781 in the style of the Ottoman Turks and is en-circled by arcades, covering a large part of the city built by the Crusaders 500 years previously. Visits by appointment; tel: (04) 991-303.

ARMED FOR ARMAGEDDON

The *Book of Revelations* states that the final battle of mankind, Armageddon, will take place on the plains around **Har Megiddo**, a town on the floor of the Jezreel Valley east of Haifa in the Galilee area.

Below: *Caesarea's Roman amphitheatre is remarkably intact.*

Crusader City ★★★

Situated across the street from the mosque, the Crusader City is dark, damp and decidedly eerie. The vast Entrance Hall is adorned with 800-year-old frescoes, and leads to the cavernous **Crypt of St John**, where the knights would hide from attackers. This crypt was later adopted by Al-Jazzar as his own escape route should Napoleon break down his defences. Because of the danger of collapsing ceilings, only one part – the Hospitaller's Quarter – is open to visitors. Open 08:30–17:00 Sunday–Thursday; 08:30–14:00 Friday.

Above and below:
Surprising details, ancient and modern, at Caesarea.

Municipal Museum ★★

Located in an old Turkish bathhouse, the nearby museum gives a good grounding in local Crusader and Islamic history, with archaeological exhibits and ancient weapons.

CAESAREA

One of Israel's most beautiful archaeological sites, Caesarea's archways and colonnades seem to go on forever, warm sandstone contrasting with the dazzling Mediterranean Sea. Crumbling walls and tumbled pillars jut out into the water and some of the ruins are actually submerged. Caesarea was built in 22–10BC by **Herod** in his usual lavish style and dedicated to Augustus Caesar, emperor of the time. The city had a reputation for violence, and the massacre of 20,000 Jews here sparked off the first uprising against the Romans in AD66.

In the fourth century, Rome fell and a Christian community thrived in Caesarea, before Arab armies invaded in 639. Crusaders arrived in 1101 and made off with what they believed to be the Holy Grail. Muslims later pillaged the city and left it to rot, while sand dunes and water gradually covered its once-majestic buildings.

Excavations in the 1950s led to the restoration of some of the magnificent buildings. You can see the massive **aqueduct**, a stunning **Roman amphitheatre**, the **hippodrome** and sundry Crusader remains. Open 08:00–16:00 daily; 09:00–15:00 Friday.

> ### ARTISTS' HAVEN
>
> A short drive or bus journey to the south of Haifa is the charming artists' colony of **Ein Hod**, a village where every other house is an art gallery. Ein Hod was started in 1953 and is a pretty collection of Moorish-style houses set amongst olive trees. Wander round the narrow streets admiring the work or browse for prints in the many shops. At the village centre, the Janco-Dada Museum houses the more prestigious pieces. It is open 09:30–17:00 Monday–Thursday, Sunday; 09:30–16:00 Friday. Closed Saturday.

Haifa at a Glance

Haifa is warm and sunny **all year round**, although the summer months of July, August and September can become very humid.

Haifa is approximately an hour's drive from Tel Aviv along a fast coastal road. **Buses** run regularly from Tel Aviv and Jerusalem. There are also good **rail** services from Tel Aviv, and *sherut* to Tel Aviv, Jerusalem, Tiberias and Akko. Haifa's **airport** is served by Arkia, Israel's domestic airline, with international flights to Amman in Jordan which is only 30 minutes away. Haifa is also a major port with **passenger shipping services** to several European cities.

Visitors have quite a wide choice of transport here. There's a good **public transport system**, Israel's only subway – the Carmelit – which goes from the old city and port up to Central Carmel; for sightseers, a **cable car** goes up the mountainside. For the energetic, the tourist board has marked four colour-coded **walking trails**, the Thousand Steps Paths. Start at the top of the mountain and walk down, rather than the other way round.

New, luxury hotels are springing up everywhere as Haifa gears itself up to be a major business travel destination. The best place for visitors to stay, however, is Carmel Centre, which is close to the shops and has panoramic views of the city.

LUXURY

Dan Carmel, 85–87 HaNassi Avenue, Haifa 31060, tel: (03) 520-2552, fax: 548-0111, www.danhotels.com Five-star hotel near Central Carmel close to shopping, zoo and parks. Swimming pool and health club.
Dan Panorama Haifa, 107 HaNassi Avenue, Haifa 34632, tel: (03) 520-2552, fax: 548-0111. Located in Central Carmel with dizzying views of the city below. Panorama Shopping Centre next door.
Dan Caesarea Hotel, Caesarea, tel: tel: (03) 520-2552, fax: 548-0111. Resort hotel on the coast with Israel's only golf course.

MID-RANGE

Beit Oren Guesthouse, Kibbutz Beit Oren, Carmel National Park, Haifa 30044, tel: (04) 830-7444, fax: 823-1443. Kibbutz hotel on Mount Carmel, some 17km (10 miles) from Haifa. Swimming pool and horse-riding available.
Beth Shalom Hotel,

PO Box 6208, Haifa 31060, tel: (04) 837-7481, fax: 837-2443, www.beth-shalom.co.il Small, comfortable three-star in Central Carmel, near shops and nightlife.
Carmel Forest Spa Resort, tel: (04) 830-7888, fax: 832-3988, www.isrotel.co.il This resort is part of Isrotel chain. Health and beauty packages.
Shulamit Hotel,
PO Box 7060, Haifa 34676, tel: (04) 834-2811, fax: 825-5206. Four-star hotel on Mount Carmel surrounded by pine gardens.

BUDGET

B & B in Haifa, Haifa Tourist Board, 106 HaNassi Avenue, Haifa, tel: (04) 837-4010, fax: 837-2953 (bed and breakfast central booking address). Accommodation is with local families and in small guesthouses.

Haifa has a great choice of restaurants and a lively night-life. Wander through Wadi Nis Nas, the Arab Quarter, in the early evening and soak up the atmosphere. Crowds of office workers visit the falafal cafés on their way home for a snack and the air is thick with delicious aromas and the sights and sounds of the *souqs*. **Hazenim** and **Mishel**, falafal shops on opposite sides of the main road, vie for the title of the best falafal establishment in Israel.

Haifa at a Glance

Nightlife tends to be aimed at the locals and there are several bars with music in addition to nightclubs. The 24-hour 'What's on in Haifa' hotline is the best source of information. Worth a visit is the entertainment complex at the brand new convention centre on the seafront, with a multi-screen cinema, some designer shops and a couple of newly opened theme restaurants.

LUXURY

Dolphin, 13 Bat Galim Avenue, Haifa, tel: (04) 852-3837. Smart seafood restaurant.

Karyola, 117 Solerot Moriak, tel: (04) 826-5827. Mediterranean specialities.

MID-RANGE

Abu Tusf, 1 Ha-Meginim Street, tel: (04) 866-3723. No-frills but excellent salad bar.

Nof, 101 Ha-Nassi Boulevard, tel: (04) 835-4311. Kosher Chinese food.

BUDGET

The Bank, 119 Ha-Nassi Boulevard, tel: (04) 838-9623. Stylish sidewalk café and popular meeting place.

Yotvata, Bat Galim Promenade (at the cable-car station), tel: (04) 852-6835. Popular vegetarian restaurant with produce straight from

the kibbutzim.

Hakadarim, Zamir Beach, Haifa, tel: (04) 851-2018. Relaxed beach restaurant with Middle Eastern cuisine.

Jacko Seafood, 12 Hadekalim Street, Haifa, tel: (04) 866-8813. Good seafood venue in the Turkish market. Open for lunch only.

Kapulsky, Panorama Centre, Haifa, tel: (04) 864-5633. Popular coffee shop in the Panorama shopping centre.

TOURS AND EXCURSIONS

Tour Operators in Haifa
All tour operators feature trips to Jerusalem, Tel Aviv, Akko, Caesarea and further afield.

Egged Tours, 4 Nordau Street, Haifa, tel: (04) 854-9555.

Mitzpa Tours, 1 Nordau Street, Haifa, tel: (04) 867-4341/2.

Carmel Touring, 126 HaNassi Avenue, Haifa, tel: (04) 838-2277 or 838-8882.

Society for the Protection of Nature in Israel (nature trails), 18 Hillel Street, Haifa, tel: (04) 866-4135, fax: 866-5825.

USEFUL CONTACTS

Car Rental
Eldan, tel: (04) 837-5303.

Taxi Hire
Kavei Hagalil, 11 Berwald

Street, Haifa, tel: (04) 866-4444/6 (taxi and *sherut*). Amal Taxi, tel: (04) 866-2324. Kavei Ha-Galil, tel: (04) 866-4444.

Sherut
Amal, tel: (04) 866-2324. Aviv, tel: (04) 866-6333.

Bus Information
Urban lines, tel: (04) 854-9131. Inter-urban lines, tel: (04) 854-9555. Haifa Central Bus Station, tel: (04) 854-9486/8.

Carmelit Subway Information
Open 06:00–10:00 Monday–Thursday, Sunday; 06:00–15:00 Friday; and from 06:00 to half an hour after sundown Saturday, tel: (04) 837-6861. The Carmelit stops at the following places: Kikkar Paris, Solel Boneh, Ha Nevi'im, Masada, Golomb and Gan Ha'em (Carmel Centre).

Tourist Information
Old Acre Development Company, www.akks.org.il Peri, tel: (04) 841-6666. Sa-Gal, tel: (04) 876-3901. 48 Ben Gurion Avenue, tel: (04) 853-5606, www.tour-haifa.co.il

Arkia Israel Airlines Ltd, 80 Aa'atzmaut Street, Haifa, tel: (03) 524-0856.

Train Information, tel: (04) 830-3133, **'What's on in Haifa' hotline**, tel: (04) 837-4253.

Travel Tips

Tourist Information

There are **Israel Government Tourist Offices** in 11 European cities including London. There are also offices in South Africa (Johannesburg), Japan, Korea, Australia, and in North America, in New York, Chicago, Atlanta, Dallas, Los Angeles and Toronto. In Israel, most major towns have a **Tourist Information Office**: Jerusalem: Jaffa Gate, tel: (02) 628-0382; Eilat: Arava Highway Corner, Yotam Road, tel: (07) 637-2111; Haifa: 48 Ben Gurion Boulevard, tel. (04) 851-2208; Tiberias: HaBanim Street, The Archaeological Park, tel: (06) 672-5666; Ben-Gurion International Airport, tel: (03) 971-1145, www.infotour.co.il

Entry Requirements

Travellers to Israel need a valid passport. Check with the Israeli Embassy whether a visa is required. Citizens of most countries, including Australia, Canada, South Africa, the United Kingdom and the USA are issued a visa on entry. Length of stay with a normal tourist visa is three months. Transit visas are issued for five-day stopovers in Israel and cruise passengers will be

issued with a landing card. If you have quite a few Arabic stamps in your passport, prepare to be questioned. If you are planning to visit Arab countries, get your Israel stamp on a loose piece of paper. Israel has a limited number of entry points. By air, these are the **Ben-Gurion International Airport** and **Ovda Airport** near Eilat. The main **sea ports** include Haifa, Ashdod, Eilat and Tel Aviv. **Land borders**, details of which are subject to change, are at the Allenby Bridge, Arava, the Jordan River, Rafiah, Nitzana and Taba. Exit fees are payable at the land border crossings, as are entry fees into Jordan and Egypt. Anyone entering Israel from the Gaza Strip is also required to clear Israel immigration at one of four checkpoints.

Allenby Bridge, border checkpoint for Israel and Jordan, open 08:00–00:00, Sunday–Thursday; 08:00–15:00, Friday. Private vehicles are permitted but not taxis and hire cars. Visitors requiring visas for Israel must obtain these before crossing at the Allenby Bridge as they are not issued here, tel: (02) 994-2626.

Arava, open 06:30–22:30 Sunday–Thursday, 08:00–

20:00 Friday and Saturday. Private vehicles permitted. Buses run from the Jordanian side to Petra. You may have to wait for two hours to cross, tel: (07) 336812.

Jordan River, operating hours as above, tel: (06) 658-6442.

Rafiah, open 09:00–17:00, tel: (07) 673-4274.

Nitzana, used mainly for goods transit to and from Egypt. Open 08:00–17:00, Monday–Thursday, Sunday, tel: (07) 655-7778.

Taba, open 24 hours a day, seven days a week. Buses run from Eilat. All tourists to Cairo, except South Africans, require an Egyptian visa from the Egyptian consulate in Eilat, tel: (07) 597-6115; take a passport photo along. Note: most borders are closed on Yom Kippur and on certain Muslim holidays.

Customs

The following items do not need to be declared. Any other items must be declared in the Red Channel at entry points. **Spirits**, up to one litre, plus two litres of wine per person over 17. **Perfumes**, up to ¼ litre per person. **Tobacco**, up to 250g or 250 cigarettes per person over 17. **Gifts** (excluding the above) up to $150 per person. **Camcorders, personal computers** and **diving equipment** must be declared and a refundable deposit paid (Visa accepted). On **exit**, tourists can claim VAT refunds for items bought from shops bearing the 'tax VAT refund' logo. Antiques (anything made before 1700) may not be exported without a written approval from the Antiquities Authority, tel: (02) 629-2627.

Health Requirements

No vaccinations are required to enter Israel except yellow fever if arriving from an infected area.

Getting There

By air

Airlines from all over the world and the national carrier, El Al, fly into **Ben-Gurion International Airport**, while El Al services and some charter flights from Europe fly into **Ovda** near Eilat. Domestic carrier Arkia flies into Eilat Airport. **Ben-Gurion International Airport**, tel: (03) 971- 0000; Ben-Gurion flight enquiries in English, tel: (03) 972-3344.

El Al reservations: El Al offers advance check-in at Ben Gurion Airport, tel: (03) 695-8614. For information, tel: (03) 971-6111, www.elal.co.il

By road

Border crossing details as above. Rented cars may not enter or leave the country. Information changes all the time as the peace process moves on, so check with the

relevant border crossing about import and export of vehicles.

By boat

A few cruise lines dock at Haifa and there is a ferry service from here to Athens. Private yachts may moor at six marinas: Tel Aviv, Jaffa, Akko, Ashkelon, Eilat and Herzliya.

What to Pack

Even for business, Israelis are fairly casual. Remember to bring sunglasses, sunscreen and a hat; swimming gear; walking shoes; and long sleeves and long trousers or a long skirt for entering religious sites. In winter, bring rainwear and sweaters.

Money Matters

The unit of currency is the **New Israeli shekel** (NIS), divided into 100 **agorot**. Visitors can bring an unlimited amount of cash or traveller's cheques into the country. Some shops accept foreign currency, although change will be in shekels. Most credit cards are acceptable. Some banks have automatic teller machines. Money can also be exchanged at hotels. VAT in Israel is currently 18%, except in Eilat, which is a duty-free zone for tourists.

Banking hours, 08:30–12:00, 16:00–18:00 Tuesday, Thursday and Sunday; 08:30–12:00 Monday, Wednesday, Friday and eve of Jewish holidays.

Accommodation

Hotels range from simple hostels to luxury establishments, graded from two to

five stars. Rates are quoted in US dollars and do not include a 15% service charge. **Kibbutz** hotels, of which there are around 280, provide a unique insight into the Israeli way of life and are mostly rural and informal. Contact Kibbutz Hotels, 1 Smolenkin Street, PO Box 3193, Tel Aviv 61031, tel: (03) 524-6161, fax: 527-8088, www.kibbutz.co.il Israel also has some 30 youth hostels, affiliated to the **International Youth Hostel Association**, tel: (02) 655-8400, fax: 655-8431, www.youth-hostels.org.il **Camping sites** are located all over the country. **Israel Camping Association**, tel: (03) 960-4524, fax: 960-4712. There are several 'special interest' forms of accommodation, too. The **Society for the Protection of Nature** has 26 field schools in rural areas, specializing in environmental protection and nature tours, tel: (03) 638-8688, fax: 687-7695, www.spni.org.il There are several Christian hostels –

contact the Christian Information Centre tel: (02) 627-2692, fax: 628-6417. Israel also has several health resorts, mostly on the Dead Sea and the Sea of Galilee.

Eating Out

Cuisine from all over the world is available in Israel. Kosher restaurants – which could be anything from Chinese food to Israeli food or international cuisine – are to be found in all hotels and in many towns. These avoid mixing meat and dairy products, so a restaurant will either serve meat dishes or vegetarian and dairy. Pork is not served in Jewish, kosher or Muslim restaurants and seafood is not sold in kosher establishments. Oriental restaurants in Israel serve Middle Eastern food, not Asian as the name might imply. This is great for vegetarians and meat eaters alike, with a huge range of *meze* (snack) dishes on offer. Travellers on a budget can do very well at the ubiquitous *falafal* stalls in every town,

where pitta bread is packed with *falafal* balls and salad. Water from the tap is drinkable in Israel but bottled water is also sold everywhere.

Transport

Air

Domestic carrier **Arkia** flies to Israel's smaller airports including Tel Aviv, Haifa, Rosh Pinna, Jerusalem and Eilat, toll-free tel: 1-800 444888, www.arkia.co.il

Road

Israel has an excellent road network and most major **car hire** firms operate here. Drivers require an international licence or a licence written in English or French. You'll also need to be over 21 and hold an international credit card to rent a car. There are plenty of repair garages and petrol stations. Petrol is cheaper than in Europe but car rental can be expensive. Parking is difficult in towns; a kerb marked with blue and white means you need a parking ticket, which can be bought in blocks from kiosks and tobacconists.

Fines and clamping are strictly enforced.

Taxis are metered and may be hailed on the streets. A *sherut* is a shared taxi, with a fixed price per passenger.

Buses

The bus network is excellent and reasonably priced. Most urban and inter-urban bus services are operated by the vast **Egged Bus Cooperative**, tel: toll free 177 022 5555. Timetables are available from tourist information offices and bus stations. To travel from Jerusalem and Tel Aviv to Eilat, you may need to book in advance. Buses do not run from sundown on Friday to sundown on Saturday and on Jewish holidays.

Trains

Israel Railways has three routes: Tel Aviv to Nahariya via Netanya, Haifa and Akko; Tel Aviv to Rahovot; and Tel Aviv to Jerusalem. Fares are cheaper than buses, and seats can be booked in advance. Trains usually have a buffet car. Like buses, trains do not run on *Shabbat* or on holidays. For information, tel: (03) 577-4000. There is one **subway** system, in Haifa, called the **Carmelit**, running from Mount Carmel to downtown every 10 min. Open 05:30–24:00 Monday–Thursday, Sunday; 05:30 to one hour before sunset Friday; from sunset to 24:00 Saturday.

Hitchhiking

Hitchhiking is a way of life in Israel and there are even special hitchhiking stations at major junctions. Motorists give

From	To	Multiply By
CONVERSION CHART		
Millimetres	Inches	0.0394
Metres	Yards	1.0936
Metres	Feet	3.281
Kilometres	Miles	0.6214
Square kilometres	Square miles	0.386
Hectares	Acres	2.471
Litres	Pints	1.760
Kilograms	Pounds	2.205
Tonnes	Tons	0.984
To convert Celsius to Fahrenheit: x 9 ÷ 5 + 32		

priority to soldiers and there can be a lot of competition. Hitchhiking is seen as a safe way of getting around but you should be aware of the risks just as in any other country.

Business Hours

Business and shopping hours are usually from 09:00–19:00 Monday–Thursday, Sunday, some closing between 13:00 and 16:00. On Fridays and holidays, shops close in the early afternoon.

Time Difference

Israel is two hours ahead of Greenwich Mean Time and seven hours ahead of Eastern Standard Time.

Communications

Israelis are avid newspaper readers and there are several dozen dailies, most with a political leaning. The *Jerusalem Post* is published Sun–Fri in English, while the *Jerusalem Report* is a bi-weekly magazine in English. There are daily and weekly publications in Arabic, French, Spanish and Russian.

TV and Radio

The **Israel Broadcasting Authority** is government-run and has two channels. There's a daily news broadcast in English at 17:30. Israel also receives **cable**, **BBC World Service**, **CNN** and **Sky**, as well as **Lebanese Middle East Television** in English and **Channel 6** from Jordan, which is also in English. The IBA also has six radio channels, including a foreign language station with regular

news in English. The army has its own radio channel, **Galei Zahal** and there are a couple of pirate stations which broadcast pop music.

Post

Post in Israel is very slow, with letters taking over a week to reach Europe and the USA. Express and Super Express services are available at a premium. Post office hours are 08:00–12:30 and 15:30–18:00 daily except Friday afternoon, Saturday and holidays. Post-boxes are red for out of town and international, yellow for local post. Telegrams and faxes can be sent from any post office on weekdays.

Telephone

Public phone booths are all over the country and take tokens (*asimonim*) or cards, which are sold at post offices or in vending machines. Most hotels have international direct dialling and the 177 toll-free number will connect holders of international phone cards to the operator. **Golden Pages** international telephone directories are published every three years. Israel is part of the GSM network for mobile phones. The code for Israel is 972 and when dialling from overseas, omit the first 0 of the area code. Area codes are: **Jerusalem** 02 **Tel Aviv** 03 **Haifa** 04 **Galilee and the north** 04 The **south** including **Eilat** and **Be'er Sheva** 07 **Ashdod** 08 **Herzliya and Netanya** 09

Israel recently switched from a six- to a seven-digit system so some numbers in tourist board brochures will be out of date. To **dial abroad**, dial 00 and the country code, omitting the first 0 of the area code.

Electricity

Electric current is 220v AC, single phase, 50 Hertz. Plugs are three-pronged round pin; most travellers will need an adaptor.

Weights and Measures

Israel uses the metric system.

Health Precautions

The biggest health risk to tourists is sunstroke, sunburn, and, consequently, dehydration. Respect the sun in Israel;

GOOD READING

Holy Bible – only in Israel does the Bible come so comprehensively to life.
Winter, Dick, **Culture Shock – Israel** (1992) Kuperard, London: Insiders' guide to politics, religion and life in Israel.
Schiff, Z and Yaari, E, **Israel's Lebanon War** (1984) Simon and Schuster, New York.
Schiff, Z and Yaari, E, **Intifada** (1990) Simon and Schuster, New York: Modern history recounted by two of Israel's best-known journalists.
Bar-Zohar, Michael, **Ben-Gurion** (1978) Delacorte, New York: official biography of the founder of Israel.

it is most dangerous between 10:00 and 16:00.

Health Services

Israel has an excellent medical system but visitors should always have private medical insurance as costs can be high. Doctors will come to hotel rooms or can be visited at an emergency room at a **Magen David Adom** (similar to the Red Cross) Hospital. For an ambulance, dial 101. **Pharmacists** operate on a rota basis, the schedule for which is published in the Jerusalem Post. Many speak English. You will need a prescription for stronger drugs.

Personal Safety

Petty crime – theft, mugging and car crime – is common but violent crime much less so. Visitors can feel very secure wandering around the

cities at night. But don't flash wealth around ostentatiously and don't leave anything valuable in a car or hotel room. **Security** is the biggest issue; report any suspicious packages and never leave bags lying around because they will be blown up immediately. Before travelling to the West Bank, be sure to check the situation with the tourist board.

Emergencies

Police, tel: 100.
Ambulance, tel: 101.
Fire Brigade, tel: 102.
There's a special tourist police division of the police force which deals with everyday matters affecting travellers.

Etiquette

Tipping in restaurants is usually 10–15%. Taxi drivers appreciate but do not expect a tip, while *sherut* drivers need not be tipped.
Conservative dress is essential for visiting religious sites. Men should wear a *kippa*, or skullcap; in many places, like the Western Wall on Shabbat, one is provided. Shoes should be removed when entering a mosque. Topless sunbathing is frowned upon.
Do not expect service with a smile in bars and restaurants; Israelis do not have the service ethic many people expect (hence the nickname *sabra*, a cactus fruit with spikes on the outside but sweet inside).
Do not expect to get anything done on a Jewish holiday (even El Al doesn't fly).

When checking in for an El Al flight or crossing borders, do not be offended by rigorous and repeated questioning; it's nothing personal.

Language

Hebrew is the official language, along with **Arabic**. **English** is learned as a second language in schools. French, Spanish, German, Yiddish, Russian, Polish and Hungarian are widely spoken. Road signs appear in Hebrew, Arabic and English.

Public Holidays and Festivals

The official holidays are Jewish holidays and Shabbat, but each religion has the right to observe its own holidays, of which there are many. Public holidays and shabbat take place from sunset to sunset. The main ones are as follows:

January or February:
Tu B'shevat
(New Year for trees)
March: **Purim**
(The Feast of Esther)
April: **Pesach** (Passover)
April/May: **Memorial Day**
April/May: **Independence Day**
May: **Lag B'Omer**
May/June: **Shavuot**
(Pentecost)
July/August: **Tisha B'Av**
Sept/Oct: **Rosh Hashanah**
(Jewish New Year)
Sept/Oct: **Sukkot**
(The Feast of Tabernacles)
October: **Simchat Torah**
(Rejoicing of the Torah)
December: **Hanukkah**
(The Feast of Lights)

INDEX

Note: Numbers in **bold**
indicate photographs